NE✗T IN LINE

A Storied Program
A Rookie Coach
The Journey Begins

SCOTT GAEDE

Author of *The Open Road: Five Years at the U.S. Open with NBC Sports*

Buttermilk Ridge Books

Buttermilk Ridge Books

Published by:
Buttermilk Ridge Publishing
136 S. 9th Street, Ste 18
Noblesville, IN 46060
www.buttermilkridgepublishing.com

Library of Congress Control Number: 2010937675

Gaede, Scott Joseph
    Next in Line / Scott J. Gaede
       p.   cm.
    ISBN 978-0-9723961-5-8

Front cover photo by Greg Rust, Xavier University.
Back cover photo by Adam Kazmierski.

Printed in the USA
Printed on acid-free paper

To my teammates; Julie, Rachel, and Caroline

Contents

Preface

As I took in the spectacle just a few feet in front of me on the floor of Lucas Oil Stadium the night of April 4, 2010, I couldn't help to be swept up in the excitement of the moment as players from Duke mobbed each other, having just won the National Championship. Seconds earlier Gordon Hayward from Butler let fly a half-court, last-second, desperation shot that, had he made, would have given Butler the win.

Let's face it; had Hayward made the shot, it would have arguably gone down as one of the greatest single moments in sports history. When I looked to the other end of the stadium and saw Hayward and his dejected teammates walking off the court I was forced to think back to the afternoon of December 18th, just a few miles away from where I currently sat, and the aftermath of Xavier's loss to Butler after a clock malfunction in the waning seconds.

At the time I was only two months into my season-long project of working with Chris on a book that chronicled his rookie season as the head coach at Xavier. It was during that hour or so after the game where I really got to see what lies at the heart of college basketball; when I saw grown men and kids cry over having just lost a basketball game.

While sitting in that dark hallway just outside of Xavier's locker room, in the basement of Hinkle Fieldhouse (which might possibly be the greatest place to watch a basketball game), it struck me that for those involved it really was much more than a game. Many of the people in that locker room that day, whether they had on a uniform, or a coat and tie, were there because of a desire to compete and challenge themselves and others around them, to be the best.

Think about it, how often can you see in one day what I was able to witness in the span of one afternoon: anticipation as the team enters the arena with the game more than two hours away, optimism in the locker room minutes before the tip, encouragement from those all around during the game, stern discipline during timeouts, sky high elation near the end of the game, then crushing defeat minutes later. Lastly, in the end you see resiliency and a renewed belief moving forward.

That game in particular came at the end of a week that saw the highest of highs for Mack and the Xavier program with a win in a classic double overtime thriller against Cincinnati in the Crosstown Shootout, then just six days later having a potential win ripped away at Hinkle.

For me, being able to watch as an innocent bystander, I was able to enjoy every minute of it, because I could, so I have to admit I was a bit bummed out to see the 2009-2010 basketball season come to an end. For Xavier, their season ended with a double overtime loss to Kansas State in the Sweet 16 in Salt Lake City. My road ended symbolically a little over a week later in Indianapolis.

I realized as the confetti rained down from the rafters of Lucas Oil Stadium that there would be no more practices, no more listening in on the huddle during timeouts, no more locker room speeches, and no more postgame congratulations. My brief time spent inside this bubble called college basketball was over.

I first approached Chris about this project last fall shortly before practice started. I had been giving the idea some thought since the day he was hired, but wanted to wait for some of the initial noise to die down before approaching him. I thought he might like the idea for two reasons; he would only have his rookie season once, and that the book might serve as a little reminder of our time spent together during the season sometime down the road. Plus it's not like we were strangers, we had known each other going back to our days together in high school at St. Xavier.

One of the best times we had together was when myself, Chris, and two others from school drove up to what was then the Hoosier Dome in Indianapolis to watch Xavier take on Duke in the second round of the NCAA Tournament. Two days before, Chris and I had both snuck out of class to watch Xavier upset Missouri to advance to the next round.

When we finally reached our seats at the stadium there was little oxygen left in the air, our seats were literally in the last row. We were closer to the roof than the court. We first sat through the second half of the Auburn/Indiana game, then, when that game concluded the entire arena emptied which gave us the chance to get all the way down behind the Xavier bench for the game. Xavier made it close, but eventually lost. For Xavier at the time, just getting into the tournament, and winning a game was considered a huge success.

A year later, Chris and I learned that we would both be heading off to school together at University of Evansville. It was an exciting time to say the least, and there are many moments that stuck out for me during our short time there together. I stayed for four years, but Chris transferred to Xavier after two.

That first semester on campus found us huddled together in each other's dorm rooms watching Bengals games each Sunday as the team made their march toward the Super Bowl that January.

Chris and the basketball team were playing well and starting to get some national recognition which was great for a school our size. That March the Aces had made it into the NCAA, beat Oregon State, and had hung with Seton Hall a little while before the Pirates finally pulled away for the win.

Chris and I roomed together our sophomore year, which happened to be the year of our infamous rabbit. For some strange reason we both decided that housing a bunny in the dorm was a great way to pass the free time, but it didn't really work out so well.

I learned during our brief time with the furry creature that rabbits can actually bite, as evidenced by the chunk of skin taken from Chris' nose on our first day after bringing the rabbit home. I also learned that rabbits are fond of hopping up onto other people's freshly cleaned laundry to relieve themselves when that person is not in the room.

Fortunately, for me, the rabbit preferred the fabric softener Chris used.

Lastly, I remember a rainy, cold November day of my senior year when I answered a phone call from Chris, and right away knew that something was wrong. As I started to ask about how things were going at Xavier, Chris cut me off and said, "I blew out my knee last night. I'm done for the season." At that time an ACL knee injury was difficult to come back from. There were plenty of players that had successful returns, and some that hadn't fared so well.

Chris persevered though, not only through that injury, but the one to his other knee as well the following summer. While those injuries may have cut short his playing career he still found a way to stay involved with the game. That involvement would bear fruit years later when he was named the head coach at Xavier.

When Chris and I finally had a rare chance to get together last year in late September I brought up the idea to him of doing a book on his first year. I had a career that went into my passion, golf, and had recently finished work on another project that detailed some of my own time "inside the ropes" working for NBC Sports.

I thought it might be fun to try and put together something similar to the John Feinstein classic *A Season on the Brink*. I told Chris that as a basketball fan I thought his first year could be a compelling read; he could come in and continue the winning tradition that now existed at Xavier, or the alternative could happen, a year of struggle. I doubted that would be the case, but I told him that I felt it would be a good story either way.

Chris gave it very little thought before saying that he liked the idea. We hammered out a few more details and a week later I found myself standing in the back of the Xavier locker room for a team meeting before a midweek practice.

The story that follows chronicles all that I was able to be part of as Chris guided the program through his first season. To say I learned a lot about how a top 25 program operates would be an understatement. I thought I knew a decent amount about college basketball having watched it for some thirty years, well, I couldn't have been more wrong.

Within a short time my vocabulary consisted of ball screens, blast cuts, seven cuts, high hands, jumping the shooter, and staying attached to your man on defense. It was during those late afternoons at the Cintas Center I witnessed what surprised me the most about the whole season; the intensity of practice. I mistakenly thought practice would be a lot of walk-throughs mixed in with certain drills. Wrong. I came to learn that practice is highly choreographed with no wasted time. The players' movement is nonstop, always rotating from one drill to the next. The only time the players get any rest is when they take a water break, but even during that down time they are shooting free throws.

The games themselves were great; the pregame locker room pep talks, the halftime meetings with the staff, the postgame celebrations, and media requests afterwards. Those were the times when I was able to see all of the hard work and preparation come together.

This project was certainly not the work of one person. A lot of different people had input throughout, and I'd like to take the time to thank each of them for their help.

First, to Chris: I couldn't have asked more of him the entire time. I wasn't sure how this was going to work, I'm not sure he did either. We had decided that we would see how the first couple of games went and then decide on whether or not to forge ahead for the remainder of the season. I think we both knew that after the week of the Crosstown Shootout and the Butler game that we had something good on our hands. Chris was more than willing with his time as we met weekly during the season to update chapters, and then later in the summer with back-and-forth edits and changes.

Chris' staff of Pat Kelsey, Travis Steele, Bino Ranson, and Brian Thornton: they made themselves available to meet anytime I had questions or needed clarification on something.

Mario Mercurio: who was often there working out the details on last minute credentials.

Strength Coach Matt Jennings: who was there after every timeout to make sure I didn't forget what was covered during timeouts.

There were others in the Xavier Athletic Department that found a way to put up with me for the last year: Tom Eiser, Brian Hicks, Mike Bobinski, and Jody Geisen. Thanks for all of your help and patience on a seemingly regular basis.

To two of my close friends: Jim Frey and Steve Wenstrup, who provided feedback, both good and bad, at various times during the season. Their comments were invaluable, oftentimes helping me organize my thoughts while assembling the layout of the book.

To my wife Julie for putting up with all of the long hours spent watching film, previewing upcoming opponents, attending practice, going to games, being away on road trips (sort of sounds like I'm turning into a coach!), and the seemingly endless hours spent typing out the words you are reading on the now fading keys on my laptop.

I hope that you enjoy *Next In Line* as much as I did working on it. After having spent a year inside the basketball program I firmly believe that this past season for Xavier, and Chris, was not a mirage, but simply a harbinger of things to come.

   –Scott Gaede

Foreword

When Scott first approached me about the idea of a book chronicling my first season as the head coach of Xavier Basketball, my first thought was, "Who the heck would want to read a book about me, besides my parents?" But, the more I thought about the idea, the more I remembered how much my dad enjoyed reading.

On a serious note, I've known Scott since our sophomore year at St. Xavier High School and knew that he'd respect the job my staff and I had to do during the season. My only concern was to make sure our players knew that they would have my total focus throughout the season regardless of the circumstances. Coach Skip Prosser, the man responsible for my career in college coaching, would always say, "It's about the kids." He was 100% right in his belief and always demonstrated that belief through his actions. As long as I continue to coach those are the words I will try and live by. This project would not change that line of thinking.

Having grown up in Cincinnati, I've been a Reds and Bengals fan for as long as I can remember. Whether it was taking the bus to a Reds game in grade school or riding my bike to the corner gas station for an Anthony Muñoz commemorative poster, I was a die hard. But until I received my first collegiate recruiting letter in 1985 from Bob Staak, Xavier's head basketball coach, I have to admit my passion for the Musketeers wasn't as rabid. It wasn't that I had another college basketball allegiance. College basketball without ESPN just wasn't what it is today.

The day I grabbed that Xavier recruiting letter from my high school coach, Coach Berning, my love for Xavier Basketball began. Watching Byron Larkin tear through Missouri in the NCAA Tournament just a year or so later cemented that feeling.

While Xavier recruited me throughout my high school years, it was never relentless enough to give me a feeling I was truly wanted by Coach Gillen. And truthfully I was fine by his decision. He had to run his program and I had to do what was best for my future. A few years later I was a sophomore forward at the University of Evansville celebrating a victory over #17 Xavier at Roberts Stadium in Evansville, IN. Being able to play at such a high level during that game and pull out the victory with my teammates was a great feeling. It was always tough to beat Xavier but on that night we did and that made me feel talented and tough enough to get the job done.

While my time at Evansville was enjoyable and provided a ton of memories on and off the floor, my basketball experience was a roller coaster of emotion. It wasn't easy the morning I walked across campus after class to meet with Coach Jim Crews but I was ready to move on. With the tough decision of transferring behind me, the hidden desire to play in my hometown was about to be realized. Coach Huggins, fresh off his first year in Clifton, and Coach Gillen both pursued me to play for their respective programs. My heart was at Xavier.

In the summer of 1990 I enrolled for classes at Xavier University and was a Musketeer. It was an exciting time. While my playing career never materialized because of knee injuries, I never regretted the decision to leave UE or the decision to attend Xavier. My Xavier teammates became, and still are, some of the best friends a teammate could ask for. Nothing ever divided us. It didn't matter that a white boy with a lawyer for a dad was part of a predominantly black team. We were Xavier's basketball team and we were tight. It's an experience you can only gain through grueling sprints at the end of a practice, monotonous study halls when the minute hand on the clock seems stuck and long bus trips after the highest of highs and the lowest of lows. Heck no, I never regretted coming to Xavier.

How ironic it was then, when in 2004, I chose to leave the bright lights of the ACC and return to Xavier as an assistant coach under Sean Miller. It wasn't an easy decision. We had Chris Paul returning for his sophomore season and were picked by many as the pre-season #1 team in the country. Many assistant coaches, friends of mine, whispered about my mistake to once again return to Xavier. As I said, it wasn't an easy decision. But for me, it was the right one.

I was never able to make any kind of mark on Xavier basketball as a player. So, who knows, maybe I can make one as a coach. It's an incredible honor to be the head coach at Xavier. Standing at the podium a few feet away from my wife Christi and our two beautiful daughters on April 15th, giving my opening statement as Xavier's Men's Basketball Head Coach was an awfully proud moment. I can only hope now that the legacy created by Staak, Gillen, Prosser, Matta and Miller will continue to grow under my leadership.

I love basketball. I love my family. And make no mistake, I love Xavier basketball. The following pages are filled with my ups and downs over the last 15 months. A lot more ups than downs. I hope you enjoy the book as much as I enjoyed living it. Go X!

–*Chris Mack*

Introduction

Boston Flee Party

The horn that signaled the end of Xavier's 2008-2009 season, a 60-55 loss to Pittsburgh in the Regional Semifinals in Boston, had just finished blaring when the questions began as to whether or not Sean Miller would remain at Xavier for another year. Many Xavier faithful though feared that this was the end of the road.

Miller, like those before him at Xavier, had come in, won consistently, then over time saw his name come up for consideration as other jobs became available at the larger conferences like the SEC, ACC, and Big 10.

One of the first schools to contact Miller had been the University of Georgia. The Bulldogs had come off of a couple of disappointing seasons and had let Dennis Felton go. The discussion never really got off the ground and fizzled.

Chris Mack said that when it became a reality that other schools were going to contact Miller, it was the first time he started to think that he might actually be in line for the Xavier job.

"During the season you hear and see these kinds of stories in the press, but you're too busy thinking about the next opponent to give it much thought. But when the Pittsburgh game was over you sort of had a sense that the next couple of weeks could be real interesting."

The next weekend Mack attended the Final Four in Detroit. Mack is at the Final Four every year to attend the National Association of Basketball Coaches year-end conference.

Most of the time Mack will go to the games on Saturday and head back home before the championship game on Monday. Most fans would kill for a chance to go to this event just once, but Mack has a little bit of a different take, "I've been to so many Final Fours as a spectator over the years. Now it's tough sitting there time after time knowing that's where you're attempting to take your own team. I may take my wife Christi to the semi-finals on occasion, but I'd just as soon sit home and watch it on TV."

By the time Mack had arrived in Detroit the whispers were getting louder about Miller leaving. As the NCAA Tournament was coming to an end, many of the larger schools were using the big final weekend as a platform to announce changes to their programs.

Miller's name seemed to keep coming up at every turn, but nothing had happened yet. Mack said that even though it appeared crazy in the media, he felt like things were actually pretty calm since Miller really didn't have anything to say about leaving.

That changed on Saturday morning. Miller had approached Mack in the lobby of their downtown hotel and said that Arizona called and wanted Miller to come out to Tucson on Sunday to enter into discussions about becoming their next head coach. Miller told Mack that he was intrigued enough to go and listen, but told Mack that "It's very preliminary, but I think I have to listen at the very least."

Even though Miller was saying that he might stay, Mack prepared for the alternative. As Mack was headed over to Ford Field for the first semifinal game between Michigan State and Connecticut, he stopped in his tracks and told his dad, Tom, and brother-in-law, Adam, that he was going to take a pass on attending.

Mack told his dad about what Miller had said that morning and he felt that if Miller did take the job, it would happen pretty quickly, meaning Xavier would do likewise and quickly commence a search for their new coach as well. Mack was pretty confident that, given his track record, he would be on the list of candidates. With that being the case, Mack felt like it was in his best interests to start putting on paper some of his ideas and thoughts for how he would run the program. When Mack made it back to his hotel room the enormity of the possibility started to hit him.

"It really got my blood pumping when I started thinking about the possibility that I could be the next head coach at Xavier in the very near future."

Mack was so engrossed in organizing some of his thoughts, he said, that he didn't even have the Final Four games on TV.

When Sunday morning dawned, Mack left early and headed to Cleveland where he took in a Cavaliers game against the San Antonio Spurs then headed back to Cincinnati where he would continue to think through some of his ideas and wait to hear the result of Miller's initial meeting with Arizona.

Later that night Miller called.

He told Mack that overall things had gone well, but were very strange. Miller had yet to see campus. Miller said that Arizona Athletic Director Jim Livengood met Miller's plane in New Mexico. From there they proceeded to go out into the desert to an undisclosed location and talk.

The reason for all of the secrecy was probably due to the fact that Livengood had tried to hire Tim Floyd, who had coached at conference rival USC. Floyd was offered the job, but in the end, had a change of heart. It was probably a blessing in disguise for Arizona fans; since Floyd's departure at USC there had been NCAA infractions that had sanctions placed on the team. Regardless, at the time, there was frustration with how Livengood was handling the search.

Mack hung up, thinking that after having traveled all the way out west, and having not even seen campus, Miller would more than likely turn the job down. Since Arizona seemed to be the one school that was hot for Miller, it seemed that if this offer fell apart, Miller could be back at Xavier, and things would return to normal.

Mack was told differently at 5 a.m. the next morning when he was roused from his sleep by Mario Mercurio, the Director of Basketball Administration at Xavier, who told Mack that Miller and Arizona had continued talks late into the evening, and Miller was starting to show some interest. Later that same day Mack got a call from Miller asking Mack and the rest of the staff to be at Miller's house by 1pm. Mack immediately knew what the meeting was for; Miller would be telling his staff that he was leaving. Mack's thought was confirmed when he got to Miller's for the meeting and a teary eyed Amy Miller opened the door, welcomed him in and gave him a hug. When all of the staff had arrived Miller told them that he had accepted the job at Arizona, effective immediately.

Miller told Mack that he would love to have him at Arizona in the event that he did not get the Xavier job. It went without saying that Mack was going to be a near-frontrunner for the job, and that Miller would offer whatever he could to make it happen, but would welcome him out west in the event Xavier went elsewhere.

As Mack left Miller's house he didn't have time to mourn the loss of a good friend and mentor, he had to work quickly to finalize his overall vision and plan for the upcoming interview. Athletic Director Mike Bobinski would move quickly, and did so, when he told Mack that they would be meeting within the week.

Since Mack and Bobinski knew each other already, Mack had the sort of awkward task of asking whether or not he should wear a suit. "Looking back now it was sort of amusing, but we knew each other so well, it was sort of like 'ok, I know that we have this interview for this very important position, should I wear a suit or not?'"

Bobinski assured him that since there was some familiarity they would keep it informal. The meeting would be held in the conference room next to Miller's old office on Wednesday at noon, Mack would be prepared.

When Mack retreated back to his hotel in Detroit a few days earlier he had begun to outline what he would later call his "Nine Point Belief" on how he planned to continue the track record of success Xavier had experienced in the past as the program's new head coach. Mack knew that during most interviews where coaches are coming into programs as a new hire, the odds are the candidate is replacing someone because of poor results. Due to that fact, many candidates launch into how they will do everything different from their predecessor in order to improve the program's image and record.

Further, Mack knew that Xavier didn't want to necessarily hear that from someone. Mack figured the administration would be open to some fresh new ideas, but overall nothing was seriously broke at

Xavier, why fix it. Having had the luxury of already knowing Bobinski, Mack knew that an important element the new coach needed to bring in was one of continuity and not so much change. Mack agreed, and it was this basic philosophy that served as the foundation for his plan.

Going into the interview Mack said his plan of attack was to be the first to talk because he had so many salient points he wanted to make and he didn't want to forget anything. Mack felt that this approach could answer most questions that Bobinski would have. As the two sat down in the conference room, Mack slid a copy of his binder across the table. Mack told Bobinski what an honor it was to be considered for the position and that he would like to take a few minutes to outline why he was the man for the job. Bobinski, inwardly impressed from the outset, was eager to hear what Mack had to say.

With most of the formalities out of the way Mack launched into the most important presentation he would ever give, one he believed that if delivered properly, could make him the next head coach at Xavier.

Point One – Keeping the Core

Mack knew that he was arguably the best choice to help keep Xavier's existing talent in place. He had worked with, and/or recruited most of the players on the roster, and felt that the rapport he already had would help everyone get through the transition.

Getting the players to buy in to the new coach and new system was the most critical factor for Xavier continued success, which is why Mack wanted to present this point first.

Point Two - The Xavier Way

Over time, a culture had developed in the Xavier program that obviously produced results when it came to playing in March. Xavier had built a track record of recent success that led to an Elite 8 finish in 2008 and another Sweet 16 run a few weeks prior. Mack believed in this culture with every ounce of his being, and so did the players. Maybe more important was the fact that the players knew Mack believed in the system.

Mack stressed to Bobinski how this would serve as a benefit to the team moving forward. Lastly, Mack pointed out, the Xavier Way was not something that other candidates could bring in from elsewhere.

Point Three - The Xavier Mission

This point was predicated on Xavier developing not just basketball players, but students, and people as well. Mack elaborated how he preached, practiced, and lived this ideal in front of the team for years. Xavier has a small, unique atmosphere that is not for everyone, and Mack knew how to continue to feed the system the type of players they needed in order to continue the success Xavier had had on and off the court.

Point Four – Basketball Identity

Mack next spoke about the type of program he wanted to lead. Mack demonstrated how he would draw on past experiences from a plethora of coaches.

As a player for Jim Crews at Evansville, Mack learned mental toughness and discipline, but also learned that he wanted to treat players with a higher level of respect and dignity.

As an assistant under Skip Prosser at Xavier and Wake Forest, Mack saw what it meant to have a broader perspective for your players beyond the game and how to develop a close knit coaching staff, but wanted to instill a more consistent system on the floor.

Lastly, as an assistant under Sean Miller at Xavier, Mack gained a tremendous understanding of the x's and o's of the college game and inherited the thick skin he would need in order to survive the day to day pressures of the job, but wanted to bring a higher level of organization to all facets of the program.

It was through this point that Mack drove home the main tenet of his entire presentation; that he was not going to change who he had become, that he had to continue to be true to himself, but in doing that he could still deliver the same message to his players that they had become accustomed to hearing. This would enable Mack to not only continue the success Xavier had, but position the program for an even higher level of expectation.

Point Five – Coaching Staff

Mack told Bobinski that he was a big believer in not being the smartest man in the room, but having the smartest room of people with which to work. The development of that room started with Pat Kelsey who was currently at Wake Forest. Mack felt that Kelsey brought an intensity and dedication to hard work that was unrivaled, and had a proven track record as a top recruiter when one looked at the roster of talent he had gathered at Wake Forest.

Mack would stay inside the program for three more hires; Travis Steele, Brian Thornton, and Mario Mercurio. Steele, who was to be named Mack's second of three assistant coaches, knew the Xavier system inside and out, and had additionally developed a great relationship with the team's soon to be best player in Jordan Crawford, whom Steele had befriended when both were at Indiana University. Thornton was a Xavier guy through and through. He was a former Xavier standout, a quick learner, and was the perfect candidate when it came to being a mentor to players. Thornton would be named the Director of Basketball Operations, the same position Mack had held ten years prior. Mack gave little thought to keeping Mario Mercurio on board. To put it simply, in Mack's mind, Mercurio was the best in the nation at what he did.

Point Six – The Bridge to Xavier Past and Cincinnati

College programs oftentimes thrive on the involvement of past players in the program, but that connection had diminished due to hiring of outside staff at Xavier. Past players like David West, James Posey, Aaron Williams, Brian Grant, and Tyrone Hill all knew Mack, and with some of that group considered close friends, Mack knew he could count on those relationships to bring this group back into the fold.

Mack also had connections to other Xavier alums like Ralph Lee, Darnell Williams, Richie Harris, Walt McBride, and Sherwin Anderson, former players that made up the inner circle of basketball cognoscenti in Cincinnati. That point alone would certainly prove helpful when it came to recruiting top level talent in Xavier's backyard. Lastly, having grown up in Cincinnati, Mack had the contacts necessary among the movers and shakers in the community and the media to be constantly selling the program.

Point Seven – The Xavier Vision

Mack spoke of moving the program to the next level. Programs like Memphis had been to the National Championship game two years prior giving schools like Xavier the belief that competing at that same level was possible. Under his leadership Mack would begin to cultivate an attitude that spoke of Xavier as a program that would have every opportunity, and right, to play in the Final Four. Competing throughout the year on a national basis and continuing to have success within their own conference, the Atlantic 10, would lay the foundation for this to happen.

Point Eight – The Plan and the Philosophy

Mack's personal philosophy regarding player development consisted of three things; the 360 degree total development of players, a systematic approach to recruiting, and a passionate belief in the current defensive and offensive system. The program would primarily practice this "360 degree" mentality in four areas; academics, off the floor life skills, on the floor basketball skills, and developing full knowledge of each player's at home support system. The systematic approach to recruiting began with an organized overall system that had equal involvement from all on the staff, and ended with a common belief in what type of player would fit in best at Xavier.

Mack stressed to Bobinski that little would change on the defensive side of the ball; Xavier had primarily been a man to man half court defensive team which yielded positive results over time. Offensively, Mack pointed out that there would be a few wrinkles in the overall system. Since the current lineup was going to be a bit smaller, Mack wanted to conduct a more up-tempo style that emphasized pushing the ball up the floor quickly on each possession.

Point Nine – Established Trust

Mack and his staff would be able to deliver unmatched continuity for the program. Something other outside candidates would be unable to duplicate. Mack made it clear to Bobinski what he would need from him; a clear line of communication on all news, good or bad. Mack was forthright and honest when he told Bobinski that he might not have all of the answers, and would look to Bobinski for advice from time to time. Lastly, Mack felt that he understood the existing dynamics of Xavier's Athletic Department. Around the office it was referred to as having a "fourth floor understanding", which not only denoted the department's location on the fourth floor of the Cintas Center, but more importantly spoke about the understanding of treating people like family. Xavier is a small school, and getting along with co-workers and different factions within the athletic department was vital.

Mack's binder had the desired effect. It left no stone unturned and left Bobinski with few questions. Bobinski told Mack that they were nearing the end of their search and that he would be back to Mack in a day or so.

Mack felt energized when he left the Cintas Center that afternoon. As he headed home to prepare for an Easter weekend trip out of town with the family to Louisville, Mack rehashed most of what he had said and felt that in retrospect there was not much he left out. Mack said that, "I felt like I prepared as best as I could. I did everything in my power to get the job, and felt that if it didn't come down my way there was nothing else I could have done."

Mack had an opportunity to meet with Boston University while in Boston for the NCAA East Regionals a few weeks earlier. But without true East coast ties, Mack never felt comfortable that he would have much shot. The job ultimately went to Pat Chambers, so for Mack, his head coaching possibilities were down to one.

Two days later Mack received a text message from Bobinski asking Mack if he could meet for lunch the next day back in Cincinnati. Mack responded, "How about breakfast?"

"I think I knew at that point it was mine. I felt that we wouldn't be sitting down to share a meal if the answer was going to be no."

Mack told his wife Christi what was happening, and the next day headed back up I-71 from Louisville to meet Bobinski at a local restaurant, John Phillips in Crestview Hills, on the Kentucky side of the river. Shortly after being seated Bobinski got to the point, "Chris, I have completed my search for our next head coach and would like

23

to tell you that I am going to recommend you to John Kucia and Father Graham."

Kucia is the Administrative Vice President and Father Graham is the President.

There was one catch; neither Kucia nor Graham were in town, so the recommendation was not going to take place until a few days later. Bobinski asked that Mack keep it quiet until then. The rest of the lunch was going over pressures of the job, and all of the demands and responsibilities of running a top-25 program.

When Mack and Bobinski parted, Mack took a few minutes to gather himself in the car before calling his wife. Mack was stunned. He had certainly put in his time over the past decade and was prepared to take on the task that lay ahead of him. Mack hit the steering wheel a couple of times and yelled, "I'm the head coach at Xavier! Yeah, yeah yeah!"

Mack finally gathered himself and called Christi to tell her that the offer had been extended, but would not be official until Kucia and Graham returned to town next week. Even though things looked good at that point, it would not be official until Kucia and Graham agreed with Bobinski's decision.

Christi talked about her emotions that day, "It was exciting to finally have the offer given. For me the last week or so had been so trying because the mother in me had taken over and I was in limbo not knowing if we were uprooting and leaving for Arizona, or staying at home in Cincinnati.

"What was harder though, was keeping the whole thing under wraps until the offer was made official. You wanted to jump up and down and let it all out, but we couldn't, at least not for a few more days."

When Kucia and Graham got back to town and signed off on Bobinski's recommendation, the offer was finally official.

Word started to leak to local media outlets that Xavier was going to name Mack as their next head coach any day. Mack's mom, Bonnie, had been hearing the reports on the news, but had not spoken to her son yet. Later in the day Mack finally called his mom to tell her the news.

Bonnie said, "When Chris called, I was so excited I had to sit down on the stairs and take a deep breath. He said to me, 'Mom I know that you are hearing a lot of reports on the news today about me being hired as the head coach, but I don't want you to believe everything you are hearing...there appears to be a snag.'

"There was a slight pause while I held my breath before Chris finally laughed and said, 'Just kidding mom, you're talking to the new head coach at Xavier!' It was such a rush of emotion; I was so proud of what he had accomplished, and so happy for him at the same time. I felt that he was the right person for the job, but I had this question that kept tugging at me during the whole process that had me wondering if Xavier wasn't going to go in the direction of someone that already had head coaching experience. In the end though, they went with Chris.

"I don't think it really hit me though until a few weeks later when I would hear on the radio about 'The Chris Mack Show', or when I saw him on a billboard. That's when the reality of it all set in."

Bonnie said that was also when a nervous pit in her stomach settled in, and would remain there all during the season, "I knew he was up to the challenge. Chris has always been so competitive. When he was younger his teachers told me that we needed to dial back his competitiveness, but how are you supposed to do that? It was just part of his makeup. I remember that when he was a freshman at St. Xavier he went out for soccer and baseball, and was cut from both. Then sophomore year he went out for soccer again, this time at goalie, and was cut. He was devastated. But it never got him down, he always recovered. I knew he would be ok in the job he was about to take on because of that spirit, that attitude.

"I knew it was probably going to be harder on me than him in the coming year because I was going to see firsthand the success of one of my children being played out in front of me on many nights. In Chris' profession you're measured on wins and losses, it's pretty black and white. I knew that concept would take some getting used to."

Mack's dad, Tom, was a bit more reserved, "I just thought that he was the logical choice. I was so confident that his experience to that point, both in and out of the program, had him ready for the job. When it came to pass though, I was just so thrilled for him and Christi. Like Bonnie, I was nervous when the season finally started, but I think that the confidence that Chris showed on the court every night rubbed off on me, so I settled down a bit as the year progressed."

On April 15th a press conference was held in the Conaton Board Room on the Xavier Campus in which Mack was to be formally introduced as the next head coach at Xavier University. In front of friends, family, and players, Mike Bobinski stood at the podium and expressed his excitement at the new hire and commented that he looked forward to working with Mack in the coming years. Bobinski next spoke the words that Mack had been dreaming to hear for a long time, "I would now like to introduce to you the new head coach at Xavier University, Chris Mack." As thunderous applause filled the room, Mack shuffled through the papers of his prepared speech, and before looking up to address the crowd said to himself, "here we go." The following is the transcript of Mack's address to the media that day:

Before I get started I would be remiss if I didn't thank a few people who have made this once in a lifetime opportunity possible. First, I want to thank Mike Bobinski for believing in me, our way of doing things and in our shared vision for the future. You don't get placed on the Men's NCAA Tournament Selection Committee through a lottery.

Mike and I had lunch the other day and it was so ironic to hear that in a day when coaches are so in tune to lining themselves up with certain people, and posturing for jobs and angling, I made my mind up years ago that it just wasn't me.

I was going to stand on my own two feet, put my head down and go to work and let the chips fall where they may. I've always been raised that you do the job you have to the best of your ability, and that you will be rewarded. Mike affirmed that belief and it's ironic that he was raised almost the exact same way.

Thanks Mike for believing in me based on my performance.

Secondly, I'd like to thank both John Kucia and President Father Michael Graham for their trust in me as the leader for this nationally recognized program in college basketball and my alma mater. I guess not skipping your history class, Father Graham, 19 years ago stuck with you. Thank you.

To the many friendly faces in the Xavier athletic department and the Xavier campus as a whole, I'm honored to represent us as we move forward in the world of college basketball.

And as we move forward I can't help but think of the two people whose lives were spent personifying Xavier and its spirit. Father James Hoff and Coach Skip Prosser helped make Xavier what it is today through their vision, their passion and their integrity. My hope is that I can continue on in a way that would make each of them proud of this place they called home.

I want to thank my wife Christi for supporting the long hours which are bound to get longer, the missed days and nights at home and the understanding she possesses thru the ups and downs of a never ending season. To Bugs and Bops (my little girls), I'm so excited that they'll be able to keep seeing the Blue Blob and the Musketeer even if they scare the heck out of you now. They won't in time.

To my mom and dad, sister Carrie (Adam) and brother Tim who's serving over in Iraq, thanks for your love and support thru [sic] all the years. What an amazing sense of pride I have to coach the program I played for in front of my friends and family.

To the players in our program, Thank You! I know that nearly each and every one of you expressed your desire for me to be your coach to Mr. Bobinski and the powers that be. But, I don't want to thank you for that as much as I want to thank you for being a good listener, a great teammate, a coachable guy that goes to class and does things the right way.

As I told Mr. Bobinski during the interview process, I felt it was so important for guys like Derrick and Jason to be able to enjoy their senior years in a system and style of play they have total belief and total confidence in. Again thanks to the players for your support. Do what we do! It's going to be fun!

To the past Xavier greats, some of which were former teammates, thank you for the memories, for the support and for being a part of tremendous basketball tradition.

A couple days after the interview, when Mike texted me to see if we could meet for lunch, I hit him back with a "how about breakfast" text? No coach in the country could be prouder, more excited and more ready to take Xavier Basketball to greater heights. As I told my wife Christi the other night, I have seen Xavier Basketball from every possible vantage point.

AS A FAN: In 1982 I attended my first Xavier game and watched Anthony Hicks drop what seemed like 40 points in Schmidt Fieldhouse or in 1987 when I watched Xavier beat Missouri and a band aided Derrick Chie-

vous in the 1st round of the NCAA Tourney led by, as I call him BLark. [sic]

AS A CAMPER: In the summer of 1984 I was issued my Bob Staak Basketball camp T shirt and learned a hesitation dribble by the college version of Magic Johnson, Ralph Lee.

AS A RECRUIT: In the fall of 1987 Pete Gillen walked into my living room with a portable VCR and showed a hi lite [sic] film that included that same Missouri win and included a segment on Sister Rose Ann Fleming, our incredible academic advisor.

AS AN OPPONENT: Wearing the then hated sleeved jerseys of the Purple Aces of Evansville I was able to feel firsthand the competitive juices opponents feel when facing the Musketeers.

AS A PLAYER: While heartache defined my time personally as a player and as a captain here, I made friendships and won championships that have stayed with me until today. Names like Aaron Williams, Tyrice Walker, Dwayne Wilson, Brian Grant, Steve Gentry, Mike Hawkins….those were and are my guys.

AS AN ADMINISTRATOR: In 1999, When Coach Skip Prosser first gave me the opportunity to be a part of the coaching profession and coordinate film exchange, arrange travel and deal with tickets. It's an opportunity I'm eternally grateful for and only wish my mentor Coach Prosser were here to share it with me.

AS A COACH: In 2004 when I left the pre-season #1 team in the county and the game's best player in Chris Paul to return home as an assistant coach. It's been a fun ride with 4 straight NCAA Tournament appearances during arguably the greatest period of basketball Xavier's ever seen.

AND NOW, in what promises to be the most exciting role of them all, HEAD COACH of my beloved and hometown Xavier Musketeers. I think I'll enjoy this vantage point the most!!

I know people may question my head coaching experience but I've been making basketball decisions my entire life. I know my Xavier experience and my passion for this school cannot be matched and that has to count for something. Trust me when I tell you that I'm going to surround myself with the best coaching staff Xavier has ever had.

A friend of mine who is the CEO of a multi-million dollar company prepared me a bit for my talk with Mike. He said, "Chris, when you have a staff meeting, your goal can't be to be the smartest guy in the room. Your goal has to be to have the smartest ROOM. I will surround myself with coaches who are smarter and better than me in areas I need help. And as long as Mike Bobinski is in that room, I like our chances.

Xavier Basketball is about 3 things:

1) We are committed to the total development of our student athletes. It's important to me that our players and recruits know we offer and expect the total package. It's not enough to win on the court. I want kids and families who understand that and want to become better than they are. I want kids who go to class and hold the doors for their classmates. I expect it all.

2) We are committed to recruiting the best players in the country that fit that mold. I want kids that understand Xavier isn't for everyone. Graduating is an expectation. But so is working to be the best player you can be to make our team the best team we can be. Our oldest players set that example every day.

3) And finally Xavier Basketball is about ironclad belief that our system, the Xavier Way as we call it, wins championships. We are a defensive team built at stopping the ball, defending as a team at all times and playing with a passion and energy on every defensive possession of the game. These guys' value stops on defense. On offense we are a team that runs, shares the ball and has fun making plays. It's a system our players believe in, have seen results in and are willing to invest in.

I can't wait to get started. I know our players can't wait. At 6 p.m. tonight we'll have our annual banquet to close the curtain on what has been a remarkable season. But tomorrow in the Cintas Center, our team will begin working towards a 4th straight A-10 championship and many more memories for next year's banquet. Thanks to everyone for coming out.

Chris Mack would exit that stage and step into a whole new world over the next twelve months. One that would be filled with ups and downs, various challenges to overcome, and dealing with the wins and losses as he made his way through his first year as head coach. In retrospect, the year would have to have been called an astonishing success comparatively speaking; a winning record, a regular season A-10 Championship, a berth in the NCAA Tournament, and advancement to the second weekend of play.

More importantly though, Mack upheld the noble cause of preparing a group of young men with the tools necessary that would enable them to become successful later in life. Most coaches are teachers at heart, instead of a classroom they use a basketball court. John Wooden, the most decorated head coach of all time in college basketball, started out as an English teacher in Indiana before becoming the "Wizard of Westwood" on the hardwood years later.

Chapter 1

Shirtsleeves and Busted Knees

Chris Mack never did want to go to St. Xavier.

The all-boy Jesuit prep school on the northern side of Cincinnati, well known for its strength not just on the field athletically, but also academically in the classroom, held no allure for Mack who wanted to go to another school in the area, Roger Bacon. That was where all of his friends were going, and like most kids of that age, Mack's desire to spend the next four years with his boyhood friends seemed a lot better than going to St. Xavier where he knew no one.

Mack's dad, Tom, intervened. Having graduated himself from St. Xavier in 1966, Tom Mack made the decision for his son; Chris would attend St. Xavier in the fall. Once the decision was made Mack came to terms with it, and knowing that there was nothing he could do about it, decided to embrace the idea of St. Xavier and make the best of his time there, which he did.

Mack's stellar play on the freshman basketball team got the notice of varsity head Coach Dick Berning who saw enough potential that he offered Mack the opportunity to practice with the varsity team later in the season during tournament play. That experience became invaluable to Mack as the varsity team made a march deep into the state playoffs.

The season would ultimately end in what had to arguably be one of the greatest games in the history of the school; a last second loss to in-conference rival Purcell in the round of eight.

Surprisingly though, Mack was not on hand to witness the event. Playing the common role of precocious teenager, Mack had been grounded by his father for not doing his homework, and therefore was not allowed to attend the game, but instead had to listen to the game on his radio back home.

Even though Mack was a 6'3", 166 lb. skinny sophomore with no varsity experience, he made the varsity squad that year and never looked back. St. Xavier may have even been a better team the year following the gut wrenching loss to eventual state champion Purcell, but failed to advance as far in the state tournament and ended the year empty handed yet again.

All had not been lost on Mack. While getting some decent stints at playing time now and then Mack learned more from the bench on varsity than he would have throwing down 30 points or so a game on the reserve team. While he still desired to be on the floor, everyday was an opportunity to learn, "For me it was a great experience to learn Coach Berning's philosophy and understand what he wanted from me. When my junior year rolled around I was starting in my second year with coach and completely comfortable. Some of my teammates were in their first year just starting the learning process, which also put me into more of a leadership role from the get go."

Even though Mack's teams failed to have lasting success in the state tournament, Mack was flourishing as an individual player.

The summer between junior and senior years saw the advent of AAU basketball in Cincinnati which opened up the opportunity to play against a whole other level of competition that could not always be replicated locally.

"It's hard to imagine basketball today with no AAU organization, but it had to start at some point. My times spent on those teams helped convince me that I could compete and have an impact on the Division I level."

Mack was starting to get some notice from schools in the MAC conference, most notably Miami University in nearby Oxford, Ohio, who had numerous St. Xavier players on their rosters in the past. But it was Mack's AAU coach Jimmy Leon who would set his life in another direction a few months later.

Leon's day to day coaching job was at Woodward High School which had become a powerhouse in the area in the past decade. Leon's star player Milt Donald had just accepted a scholarship to attend the University of Evansville in southern Indiana under Coach Jim Crews. Crews had a growing reputation among NCAA coaches as the next possible Bobby Knight.

Crews played for Knight while at Indiana University, and had been a member of the 1976 National Championship team that went undefeated. Crews employed a style very similar to Knight's; a methodic, tough, half-court offensive predicated on ball movement and a lot of screens.

Leon began to think that this was a system in which Mack could do well and made mention to Crews that he might want to take a look at Mack in the coming months. While Mack was aware of the attention he was getting elsewhere, inside he secretly burned to play locally.

Tony Yates was the head coach at the University of Cincinnati and while he was quite aware of Mack's accomplishments, Yates showed little to no interest during recruiting. Mack only received one letter from the school, which seemed to be more of a formality with not much real interest behind it.

Across town at Xavier University, Pete Gillen showed a bit more interest, but it never really went too far beyond that. Gillen felt that Mack was a good player, but opted to recruit and sign New York native Jerome Holmes instead.

Back in Evansville, Jim Crews was starting to show more interest as fall approached, and eventually offered a scholarship to Mack. In November Mack signed his national letter of intent to attend Evansville. With the pressure of the overall decision finally settled Mack began to play the best basketball of his high school career.

At the annual Blue Chip Classic played in December every year in Cincinnati where local teams were paired against some of the best teams from around the country, Mack went on to become the MVP after pouring in 35 points and grabbing 14 rebounds in St. Xavier's win over Henry Clay. Mack would eventually go on to claim "top player in the city" honors as the season came to an end then headed off for his first year of college with all of the confidence in the world.

"Hill, you're absolutely worthless. You are never going to be a leader on this team because of your attitude and your laziness!" That phrase was one of the first Mack remembers hearing from Crews when got to Evansville.

Mack kept to himself during a break at one of his first practices shooting free throws and listened in as Crews proceeded to rip into junior forward Brian Hill about his work ethic. "I remember thinking, 'Wow, Coach is really letting Brian have it, maybe he should get his act together and do what Coach says.'"

A few weeks later Crews broke into the same diatribe, except this time it was directed at Mack, "If you think you can come in here and half-ass it like you are, you'll never see the floor during a game."

Mack explained how he felt about the comments from Crews, "At that point I understood, it all became clear, and from that point on I knew what sort of coaching style I was going to be dealing with for the next four years. It was hard coming to practice knowing you were going to get ripped to shreds, but that's what I signed up for at the time." Even though Mack's developing relationship with Crews was tenuous at best, he still found a way to forge himself into the starting lineup on a team that would eventually post a 25-6 record by season's end, then cap off the year by creeping into the Top 25 the last week of the season.

Evansville was under the radar for most of the year until mid-February when Scott Haffner poured in a school record 65 points in a televised game against conference opponent Dayton. The always attempting-to-be-humorous Mack exclaimed afterward in the locker room, "I'll never forget this game. To look back on this one day and realize that Haffner and I scored 74 points combined is really special!"

The Aces met their toughest MCC opponent, Xavier, in the conference championship game in Dayton. Evansville came up short in a losing effort 85-78, then would have to wait until the next day, Selection Sunday, to learn their fate of whether or not they would make it into the tournament.

Mack and his teammates had to wait until the final bracket was revealed to learn they had made it as an at-large bid and #11 seed in the West Region. Evansville would be taking on #6 seed Oregon State led by All-American standout Gary Payton. The game was going to be in four days at the McKale Center on the campus of the University of Arizona.

Evansville pulled off one of the more notable upsets in the first round after beating Oregon State 94-90 in overtime. Point guard Reed Crafton had a game tying three in the waning moments to force a tie. The Aces won the battle on the free throw line and after five extra minutes of play were in their way into the second round.

"Taking the floor for the first time as a player in the NCAA Tournament is an incredible feeling. After watching the tourney for all of those years growing up on television it's sort of hard to believe you are actually participating," Mack said about the game.

"The thing I'll never forget about the Oregon State game was our point guard, Reed Crafton. He was the most fearless player, and craziest person, I've ever played with. He ended up getting kicked off of our team the next year because of how wild he was, but boy did he compete, and wasn't scared of anything," Mack recalled.

"Before the game Coach Crews made it perfectly clear not to say a word to this guy named Gary Payton. Crews said any trash talk to Payton would ignite him. Pac 10 coaches had spread the word to our coaching staff. So, just as the referees are about to toss the ball up for the opening tip, what do you think Reed Crafton does as he's standing next to Gary Payton? Reed winks at all of us (his teammates), and says, 'Hey Gary, I'm about to bust your sorry ass on national TV.' That was classic Reed Crafton. Wherever you are Reed, I love you, but just so you know, Payton did score 30! I will give Reed his due though, he made the game winning three-pointer in OT to help us win the game."

Two days later, Evansville was facing #3 seed Seton Hall that dispatched their first round opponent Southwest Missouri State easily in the first round. Seton Hall jumped out to an early lead and extended it to double digits early in the second half. Evansville came all the way back to nearly force a tie when Scott Haffner's three pointer from the corner rimmed out. The Aces never got closer than that, and Seton Hall pulled away again to eventually win 87-73.

Mack and his teammates had a lot to be proud of looking back on the year; a regular season conference championship, a Top 25 ranking, a win in the NCAA tournament, and a second round loss to Seton Hall who went all the way to the finals before losing to eventual national champion Michigan.

Mack remembers the scene in the locker room after the loss to Seton Hall, "The finality of the whole thing was so much bigger than high school, especially for the seniors."

Mack and Crews were able to get along for the most part with Mack having started 17 of 30 games. "Overall I would have to say freshman year was a success, but sophomore year was a different story."

For reasons that he still can't understand to this day, Mack caught the brunt of Coach Jim Crews wrath from the opening tip the next year. The yelling, the screaming, and the name calling took a toll as the year wore on.

For Mack, it was Crews' inconsistency that confused him the most. Mack was relegated to coming off the bench against Siena after starting in the Aces' first eight games of his sophomore year. Nobody on the coaching staff had ever said anything to Mack before tipoff. A determined Mack later came in off the bench to pour in a then career high 22 points. During the ensuing Christmas break Mack started to have his first thoughts about leaving the program.

Having gotten back to a cold and empty dorm room on a gloomy, winter night Mack was staring out his window thinking about his future, "I thought I could stay at Evansville and stick it out, but the basketball experience was growing tougher by the day. No one enjoyed going to practice and basketball began to feel like a job. For something I loved so much to turn sour was depressing.

"In my mind I contemplated leaving, but we hadn't even started conference play and I was beginning to play well despite my feelings. Lastly, we were only a game under .500 and still had a chance to put together a decent year."

Everything hit rock bottom during a game in Dayton a month later.

Having trailed Dayton from the opening tip, Crews was not in a good mood. Crews was also frustrated by Dayton player Wes Coffey, whom Crews felt was crowding the ball each time Evansville tried to inbound the ball versus Dayton's full court man-to-man pressure.

During the next timeout, Crews made it clear that the next time Coffey crowded the inbound pass, he wanted his players to plant the ball in his face.

Sure enough, less than a minute later, Evansville point guard Scott Shreffler was inbounding the ball with Coffey all over him. Shreffler did as he was instructed and threw the ball right into Coffey's face.

"Right after Shreffler did that, it was like it happened so fast, the Dayton players and fans were sort of looking around wondering what just happened. The refs blew the whistle because the ball went out of bounds off Coffey and it was still our ball. Coffey backed up a bit and Shreffler got the ball in much easier the second time, but it was clear that the Dayton players and staff were not happy."

Later in the half Mack found himself standing on the end line with the ball in his hands ready to inbound against the same press. With Coffey toeing the line and a 5-second count nearing, Mack knew the ensuing result was not going to be pretty.

1..2..3..4.., Mack had little time to waste, then finally threw the ball into Coffey's face. The entire arena came unglued. When the officiating crew was finally able to separate the two teams and coaching staffs, Mack had been assessed a technical foul and quickly found himself at the center of the entire controversy.

After the game was over, Mack personally felt that Crews did not back him.

"I wasn't even on the bus when I had decided that this probably wasn't going to be the place for me. Back in December after the Siena game I made a promise to myself that I wouldn't think about making a decision until the season was over, my effort level was still going to remain at 100%, but after the Dayton game I had a hard time not focusing on my future.

"To continue to play for Coach Crews and the University of Evansville would have been tough. I wanted basketball to be fun again. Coach actually made my decision to leave an easy one."

Two months later after an 11-point loss to Xavier in the MCC finals

Chris Mack had donned the long sleeve uniform of the Purple Aces for the last time. As the two teams met to shake hands, Mack pulled Xavier player, and old high school rival Dave Minor, off to the side to tell him that he was likely going to transfer. When Minor asked where, Mack replied, "I'd love to join you." It was a brief encounter, but one that would appear to be clairvoyant a month later.

"In a lot of ways it was tough for me to leave Evansville. I made some great friends there and really enjoyed the overall experience I had there, but it was time to move on. And no, I never did like wearing those shirtsleeves!"

Mack had approached both Pete Gillen at Xavier and Bob Huggins at the University of Cincinnati about his desire to transfer. Both were willing to listen, but after a few short meetings Mack made his decision and chose Xavier.

Mack went to his father, Tom, and asked for his help during the transition out of Evansville to Xavier. When Mack told Crews about his decision to leave, Crews informed him that he would not release Mack to another school within the MCC.

Mack spoke to his dad about the roadblock. Shortly thereafter, Tom Mack, an attorney by trade, had a conversation with Crews. The release came down, and Mack was headed to Xavier.

"I don't know what my dad ever said to Crews to this day. All I know was that it worked out for me in the long run."

Mack released a statement to the press saying that he was not enjoying the experience and had lost a lot of confidence and felt it was in everyone's best interest to move on.

"Even though I was going to sit out the coming year (NCAA rules mandate that all transfers sit out for one year) I was happy. I was going back home, playing for a coach and school that I loved in the first place. It was a fresh start."

The excitement level was at an all-time high on the Xavier campus. Coach Pete Gillen had led the team to a Sweet 16 appearance in 1990 after beating top ranked Georgetown in the second round of the tournament.

Mack's first year on the squad saw the team return to the NCAA Tournament yet again. After getting past a feisty Nebraska team in the opener, Xavier lost to Connecticut in the second round.

Per NCAA rules transfers were not allowed to travel with the team, so while Mack was not able to experience the excitement of being in the tournament with his new teammates, it was still a tremendous opportunity to learn.

"I would never say that the transfer year was a waste. Even though you are dying to get out on the floor, you still have a lot of learning and growing to do as a player at that age, and there were certainly a number of things that I benefited from during the year I sat out."

During the summer of 1991 Mack began to elevate his game to another level. Playing in the Deveroe's/Purcell Summer League, which consisted of a collection of some of the area's top high school, collegiate, and pro talent, Mack dominated throughout, and earned MVP of the league.

That caught the eye of many within the basketball community in Cincinnati. It appeared that Mack had made the right decision, and for Gillen, he was going to be a solid addition to Xavier in the upcoming year.

Gillen had been impressed with Mack's dedication and leadership both on and off the court in the last year. Gillen, additionally taken by Mack's performance on the court that previous summer, named Mack as one of the team captains for the upcoming season.

When practice opened in October, Mack had not lost a beat. He continued to play well, including a 32-point performance in the team's annual blue/white scrimmage.

Everything seemed to be in place the night of the pre-season opener. Mack had taken the floor as a starter and was looking forward to finally playing in front of hometown friends and family in a Xavier uniform.

"The ball was tipped to the other team so we got back on defense. I yelled to my teammate, Jamie Gladden, I had his man who had been out on the wing and was going to go baseline. I moved over to block his path to the goal and took the charge. As soon as I planted my foot that was closest to the baseline I felt a pop. I knew something was wrong.

"At first I wasn't sure what happened. Something didn't feel right, but I thought I could shake it off when I was able to get up to walk off the court. As I made my way to the training room I kept sensing that my left knee had no stability. That was the first time I thought this could be serious," was how Mack recalled the events of that night.

It was serious. Mack was to find out that just a mere eight seconds into his Xavier playing career he had blown out his left knee by tearing the anterior cruciate ligament. Every player that had made it to the level Mack had in the game always feared an injury such as this. The list of players that never fully recovered from that type of injury was a long one.

Mack's father Tom went down into the tunnel to talk to Chris and found out what happened, "It was just a sick feeling. There was nothing I could do for him. That was tough to have to watch one of your kids go through that."

Mack's mom, Bonnie, remembered Tom coming back up and telling her what happened, "I remember sitting there and we had parents of many of the other players on the team sitting around us cheering on their own. I just felt sick to my stomach. It was so hard to sit there while others continued to watch their kids play, and mine was underneath the stands, with a dream having just been crushed. It was awful to sit through."

Mack was determined to be one of the few that would overcome.

Mack had learned that doctors performing the surgery had recently started to change the procedure which was having dramatic effects on shortening the amount of rehabilitation time, thus allowing players to get back on to the court much sooner than before.

The old procedure did not replace the ACL, but merely prevented the knee from hyperextending. The problem was, that often left bone on bone, which caused more complications down the road. High profile players like Danny Manning at Kansas, and Steve Kerr at Arizona, had opted for the new procedure, one that Mack and his family began to investigate.

In the new procedure doctors would take a graft from some other part of your body, such as the hamstring, and use this to replace the injured ligament. It was sort of like a replacement part, so the structure of the knee was unaffected. The new procedure not only allowed players to heal and get back to playing quicker than before, but it allowed for a better long term prognosis as well. Dr. Robert Heidt Jr., the orthopedic doctor for the Cincinnati Bengals, would perform the surgery. Once the surgery was performed Mack knew in all reality that the harder part of experiencing this injury was about to start, the rehabilitation, which he aggressively attacked. Mack had to idly sit by for another year and watch his Xavier teammates eventually lose to his former team, Evansville, in the semifinals of the conference championship. As a result, Xavier failed to qualify for postseason play.

Later that summer, and perhaps too eager to get back on the court, Mack decided to sign up again and play in the Devoroe's/Purcell Summer league where he had so much success in the past.

After getting over some of the expected tentativeness Mack was starting to get his playing legs back under him when the unthinkable happened, he blew out his other knee.

"Looking back now I'm not really sure how I was able to get through that. It was nearly impossible to get my mind around the fact that this (the knee) had happened again. But I never once thought about quitting. I loved the game too much. I was hoping if I could get through rehab on schedule I could be back by Christmas or early January."

Midway through the first half during an early January home game against Notre Dame, Gillen called Mack off the bench and sent him into the game. It had been a little under three years since Mack's last appearance in a regular season game.

"Even though I was glad to be back, and happy that I had completed the journey, my days of getting serious floor-time were behind me. At that point in the season the rotation had been set, and it was going to be a bit hard for me to do much in the last couple of months." Mack helped the team close out the season with a 21-4 record along with a national ranking in the AP poll.

Playing in the MCC Conference Championship in Indianapolis Mack was handed a loss in the finals by his former school Evansville, but unlike the year prior, Xavier had a good enough record to be eligible for postseason play. Xavier was back in Indianapolis a few days later after Xavier had been selected as an at-large invitee to the NCAA tournament where they easily dispatched New Orleans in the first round. That win moved them on to face #1 seed Indiana University, and legendary coach Bob Knight, in the second round.

Mack recalled, "The thing I remember most about that game was Coach Knight coming out of the tunnel a minute or two before the starting lineups were announced, and the entire stadium went crazy. I had never seen that sort of reaction for one person."

Xavier, however, was not intimidated by the partisan surroundings and pushed the number one ranked Hoosiers into the last minute of the game. Xavier made a three pointer to cut the lead to two. What happened next was, depending on whose side you were on, either very smart or very aggravating.

"As (Indiana player Damon) Bailey went to get the ball after it had come out of the basket, he just sort of slowly walked in the direction of the ball to retrieve it, all while continuing to run time off the clock.

"The referees would not start their five second count on the inbounds until Bailey had the ball in his hands. So, the clock keeps ticking until, with about six seconds left, he picks the ball up, then waits nearly five seconds to get the ball inbounded before we foul to stop the clock.

"I thought it was a smart play on his behalf, but I felt it compromised our chance to win. Ironically enough the NCAA used that play as an example when drafting a rule that would take effect the following season; all made shots in the last minute of a game would stop the clock until the ball was inbounded."

Having completed his college career, Mack found that he still had a passion for playing the game and decided to accompany an Athletes in Action squad that was making a trip though South America later in the fall. Mack played well enough during that time to get noticed by pro scouts in Europe and was later invited to come play for a pro team in Slovenia called Postojna.

"One night after one of our games, myself and some of the other members of the teams were sitting around in the locker room. It was crazy over there how many players smoked in the locker room, something you would never see in the States. Anyway, I happen to look down at my knee and see this sort of bump sticking out. I start to break out in a cold sweat wondering what might be wrong now.

"Shortly after noticing the bump, my knee starts to hurt during practice, and in games. I finally meet with the team doctors, but nobody is able to get anywhere. I speak English, they are speaking Slovenian, and no one can understand a word the other is saying. I'm thinking that something serious is going on, so I finally decided to head back to the States to have people I know and trust take a look at the knee."

To Mack's relief doctors back in the states said that the bump was nothing more than floating cartilage and would go away on its own over time. Even though this was good news, the whole event gave Mack pause about his career. The knee seemed as though it was going to be an ongoing issue, he was not getting any younger, and there were no opportunities on the horizon that were too appealing.

Mack finally came to the conclusion that it was time to move on from his playing career and get on with the next phase of his life. Surprisingly, that next phase came in the form of selling for Home City Ice in Cincinnati. Even though the job produced a paycheck it lacked a level of intensity that Mack had gotten used to from playing competitive basketball.

A short time later another opportunity came up to sell oil and other additives at a locally owned company, Vulcan Oil. "The company was great to me, but my heart was never in it. I was drawing up inbounds plays between calls. That told me where my passion was, it was basketball, not selling oil.

Mack's sister, Carrie, was a senior at McAuley and the school was looking for someone to coach their junior varsity girls' team. Mack took the job, performed well and at the end of his second season was offered the position as head coach of the varsity team at another local all-girls school, Mount Notre Dame.

Mack remained in that position for the next four years, often taking his teams down to watch Xavier practice. That move also served to keep an open line of communication with head coach Skip

Prosser who had taken over the program after Pete Gillen left to coach at Providence. Mack had remained close with Prosser whom he befriended during his playing days when Prosser had served as one of Gillen's assistants.

Shortly thereafter, Mack learned that one of Prosser's own assistants, Michael Davenport, had quit which opened up a spot on the staff. Mack quickly contacted Prosser to interview for the position.

The longer the process went on the more excited Mack got about the fact that this new position was exactly what he wanted to be doing and could hopefully send him off in a whole new direction with his life.

Mack felt confident that he had interviewed well and was the leading candidate; so naturally, he was crushed when the phone call came from Prosser notifying him that he did not get the job.

"Coach called and told me right off that he had offered the job to Mark Gaffney. I was just crushed; I thought the job was mine. I knew chances like this did not come around often, and felt like I may have missed my only chance to get into coaching on the Division I level."

Mack remained at Mount Notre Dame diligently coaching the varsity team when one day he got a call from former player Sherwin Anderson telling him that Prosser had thought of adding a position on the staff titled Director of Basketball Operations, and that Prosser had asked Anderson about Mack's interest.

Since the program continued to have success there was a growing need for a position such as this that would serve as a catch-all for various administrative and operational duties. Prosser obviously knew Mack well, and even though he passed on him for the assistant coaching position, Prosser saw Mack was strong enough in the interview and would no doubt be the best person for this new position.

Prosser felt that Mack's knowledge of the program, and organizational skills, would lend themselves perfectly to this introductory position within the program. Prosser also felt it was a great way to get Mack involved on a day to day basis with the program and to provide him with the opportunity he needed to one day break into coaching.

Mack took all aspects of the position head on, which included coordinating team travel, tickets, and running camps. Mack also became the lead contact for all recruiting visits and film exchange with other teams for scouting.

Mack found himself involved in almost every aspect of the program, and loved it, "I wanted to prove to Coach that he made a good hire and demonstrate that I had the work ethic and desire to learn that could one day serve him well on the sidelines." That approach served Mack well when Prosser moved on from Xavier after the 2000-2001 season when he accepted the head coaching position at Wake Forest.

"Coach Prosser treated the entire staff like family; he wanted everyone to go with him to Wake. One of his assistants, Mark Schmidt, was interviewing at Robert Morris, and wound up getting the job. That left a spot open on the staff which coach offered to me a short time later. When I moved up to the coaching staff that made room for Pat Kelsey to come on board and take my place in Operations".

Mack's three seasons at Wake Forest occurred during a dominating stretch for the Atlantic Coast Conference; Maryland won the national title in 2002 under Gary Williams, and Roy William's arrival in North Carolina created the foundation that would lead to a national title in 2005.

Mack had the opportunity to coach talent unlike any he had ever been around. Players such as Josh Howard, who won the ACC Player of the Year and Chris Paul, who was a freshman in Mack's last season with the Demon Deacons, are probably at the top of the list. Both players have gone on to become household names as their careers have progressed in the NBA. Wake Forest was in the NCAA tournament all three years Mack was in town, capturing a Sweet 16 appearance in Mack's final year on the staff. The team had ascended to a pre-season #1 ranking before Mack's departure.

"It certainly was a heady time. Every game in the ACC is big. We had some memorable games along the way. Playing in arenas such as Cameron Indoor and the Dean Dome were always tough, but we always looked forward to those challenges," said Mack reflecting on his time there, "I was 0-3 at Cameron, but 3-0 in the Dean Dome. I wonder how many coaches can say they're undefeated at Carolina."

Mack loved getting the chance to work alongside Prosser on a daily basis. "Coach was a very worldly person. He was well read on a lot of topics that had nothing to do with basketball. He used any and every opportunity to try and teach you things about life. He always had a family type atmosphere with his staff that just made it so special to be part of. I was crushed when I got the news of his passing; I still miss him to this day."

July 26, 2007 was a steamy, hot day in Winston-Salem. Prosser had gone out for his midday jog and upon returning to campus retired to his office where he was later found slumped over on his couch and unresponsive by director of basketball operations Mike Muse. Prosser was raced to Wake Forest Baptist Medical Center where he was later pronounced dead at 1:41.

Prosser had returned earlier in the week from an AAU tournament in Orlando. Mack was at the same event when the news broke. "Looking back now it was kind of strange because I saw Skip's son, Mark, get off his phone and quickly leave the gym. He had a sort of concerned look on his face, but I really never gave it a second thought at the time. I later realized that was when he had received the bad news," said Mack.

Mack had been sitting with Jeff Boals, a close friend of Mack's who was an assistant at Akron during the time, who answered a call on his phone. Boals hung up and looked over at Mack and said, "There's a report out there that said coach died in his office today after going jogging." Mack made a number of phone calls to try and verify what he had heard, but was not able to get through to anyone. Mack finally reached Dino Gaudio, Prosser's top assistant, and finally confirmed what he hoped was not true, that coach was gone.

Mack's mom, Bonnie, spoke about the impact that Prosser had on her son, "Chris just thought so much of Coach Prosser. I told Chris at the time that the best way for him to honor Skip and his legacy was to try and emulate all of the things that he stood for. Skip's programs were like one big family, he tried to be a mentor to everyone. Chris knew exactly what I was saying and he took it to heart. To this day I see little bits of Skip in the things that Chris does with the players and others around the team."

A service was held at the Cintas Center on Xavier campus before Prosser was laid to rest in Spring Grove Cemetery in Cincinnati.

At the time of Prosser's death, Mack had just completed his third year under Sean Miller at Xavier. Shortly after the conclusion of the 2003-2004 season Mack received a call from Mario Mercurio who was in basketball administration at Xavier. Sean Miller, who served as an assistant under Thad Matta, had just taken over the head coach position after Matta was offered the top spot at Ohio State.

Miller was assembling his staff and knew of Mack because of their time spent together in the business. Mercurio suggested Miller pursue Mack. Miller knew Mack was the type of person he wanted on his staff and asked Mercurio to contact Mack and gauge his interest level.

Mack was interested.

Mack flew back to Cincinnati where the two met at a hotel near the airport. Miller was impressed and offered Mack the job. It was a no brainer for Mack. The new position offered the chance to come back home which had enormous appeal.

Mack had just married, and his wife, Christi was also from nearby having grown up in Louisville. Both had been thinking about starting a family, and each liked the idea of their children being close to grandparents on either side of the family. Even though Wake Forest had been ranked pre-season #1 in many polls, Mack knew coming back to Xavier was the right move.

Mack said, "You know, the decision to come back to Xavier always felt right. It seemed like Xavier was always the place I came home to. I did it when I was in college, and now I was here to do it again in my professional life."

Miller's first year at Xavier was transitional; the team finished 17-12, lost in the semifinals of the conference championship to Saint Joseph's and did not go on to postseason play. The next year Xavier reeled off four straight wins in the conference tournament to gain an automatic berth into the NCAA Tournament where they would meet #3 seed Gonzaga. Armed with All-American Adam Morrison, Gonzaga proved too much and defeated Xavier 79-75. Mack spoke about that game, "Even though we lost by four, we were not ready for that stage yet. It was a great learning experience that prepared us for future success."

The next year Xavier was back in the NCAA facing Miller's former boss; Thad Matta and Ohio State in the second round. Xavier had won its first NCAA game under Miller two days earlier beating Brigham Young 79-77.

Xavier had the #1 seeded Buckeyes down fifteen points with just under seven minutes to play. Ohio State fought their way back, sending the game into overtime. OSU's experience and size was the difference as they pulled away to win 78-71.

"That was a huge game for us. Of course, there was a lot of disappointment at that time, having lost, but when you look at the team they had, which went on to lose to Florida in the National Championship, you started to realize, hey, we have a great team here that can play with the best in the country."

The next year Xavier had the talent and depth to make a run deep into the NCAA tournament that ended with an Elite 8 loss to UCLA 76-57. Mack said of the loss, "We just didn't do anything offensively the whole day that forced UCLA to do anything differently on defense. Sometimes you just lose, there's not much more to it than that.

"As a staff we never talk to the players about what is at stake. Everyone knew that if we win that one game we were in the Final Four, so there is a lot of disappointment after the loss, but it never really registered until the next weekend in San Antonio what you nearly accomplished. It just served to make you work harder the next year."

The next year saw Xavier again return to the NCAA tournament and again make it to the second weekend that ended with their 60-55 loss to Pittsburgh.

Miller had certainly raised the level of expectations within the Xavier community with back to back Sweet 16 appearances, so there was a lot of consternation when it was announced that he was leaving.

A lot of names were thrown around over the next few days as many tried to guess who the next head coach would be. When Mack was chosen, there were far more supporters than detractors, as the next chapter of Xavier basketball history was about to be written.

Chapter 2

Ok, Now It's My Turn

A recent interview in *Cincinnati Magazine* quoted Xavier Athletic Director Mike Bobinski as saying "There's every reason to believe that there may be a different dynamic here than we've had before, and that would be great with me."

The article went on to quote Mack as saying, ""For me, I firmly believe in this place. I recognize that I'm fortunate to be the head coach here. I really am. I'm not Sean Miller. I'm not Thad Matta. Ultimately the proof is in the pudding, and whether a fan takes me at my word I don't know. But I know this: I chose to be at Xavier when a lot of assistant coaches thought I was crazy to leave the ACC. That was for Xavier and for my family, those priorities haven't changed."

Mack had been well aware of the history surrounding the program long before coaching from the sidelines. Mack, and yours truly, the author, drove to Indianapolis two days after Xavier's first win in the NCAA in 1987 to see the Musketeers almost upset Duke and earn a trip to Cincinnati for a regional semifinal showdown with Indiana.

Mack had inherited a talented, but unproven, roster for his first year as head coach. It was a team that had lost three key players and a head coach, but on the flip side was returning players with some experience and a potential star in soon to be eligible Jordan Crawford from Indiana.

Derrick Brown's decision whether or not to go pro was looming over the program. Brown was a fixture on the team as a floor leader and major impact player. Brown's decision would have major ramifications either way.

"Derrick had the choice of a lifetime on his hands, I certainly did not want to rush things, but I also felt like we were sort of stuck in neutral until he decided," said Mack looking back. So, while Mack, along with everyone else, waited for the word to come down from Brown, Mack got to work bringing his staff together for the first time.

"The whole process went pretty quick. I gave it some thought ahead of time, and with two staff members, Mario Mercurio and Travis Steele already in house, and another having had ties to the program in the past in Brian Thornton, the rest of the pieces came together quickly."

Mack had worked alongside Pat Kelsey at Wake Forest and was already familiar with what Kelsey could add as the first assistant. "Pat called to congratulate me on my promotion and I replied that I was excited to hear that he may be taking the head coaching position at Appalachian State, so I was a bit surprised to hear him say that he wanted to come on board with me at Xavier. When he convinced me that this was where he wanted to be at, I jumped at the chance."

Kelsey had spent the last eight seasons at Wake Forest, and was also a former Xavier team captain. "Pat is regarded as one of the best assistant coaches in America," said Mack, "he was pursued by some of the best programs before coming to Xavier. He's going to out-work, out-hustle and out-effort the competition. Most important in my mind though, is that Kelsey embodies what Xavier stands for and believes in - the total development of our student-athletes."

Kelsey had earned the reputation as one of the nation's top young coaching talents during his tenure at Wake Forest, including three years as the director of basketball operations under the late Skip Prosser, and five years as an assistant coach under current head coach Dino Gaudio. Kelsey began his coaching career at his prep alma mater, Cincinnati's Elder High School, from 1998-2001 as an assistant coach under former Xavier guard Joe Schoenfeld. Kelsey left Elder and headed to the college ranks and Wake Forest in the spring of 2001, joining Prosser's first Deacon staff as director of basketball operations.

After three years in the DBO position, Prosser promoted Kelsey to assistant coach prior to the 2004-05 season. During Kelsey's tenure in Winston-Salem Wake averaged nearly 21 wins per year in eight seasons, earning five NCAA Tournament berths, an NIT berth, a No. 1 national ranking in two different seasons, and an ACC regular season championship. In addition to his recruiting prowess, Kelsey was also recognized as an excellent teacher and tactician in terms of player development, scouting and game preparation.

Kelsey also possessed a prior history with the Xavier program as a leader in the Xavier back-court for three seasons (1996 to 1998), helping the Musketeers reach two NCAA Tournaments. The former point guard served as team co-captain during the 1997-98 season, and was voted the team's Most Inspirational Player in 1996 and 1998.

"I just can't say enough about how excited I am to work side by side with Pat every day. Our players and program are going to reap the benefits of his involvement for some time," said Mack of his Associate Head Coach.

Having already known Travis Steele, who spent last season as Xavier's Director of Basketball Operations under former head coach Sean Miller, Mack had a rather easy decision when it came to naming his first assistant head coach. "I am a huge fan of Travis, he has such a great ability to connect with our players on every level," said Mack. "He's going to be a tremendous coach. Our players love Travis and his understanding of our system is invaluable. He'll be a relentless recruiter, a self-starter in the office, and an energetic presence on the practice floor."

Steele joined Indiana University in August of 2006, taking on the duties of the video coordinator. Steele facilitated advanced scouting of opponents, was responsible for evaluating team practices and organized prospect recruiting on a national level. After serving as the video coordinator for a season and a half Steele was promoted to the position of assistant coach under Kelvin Sampson in February 2008. In that role, he participated in recruiting, both on and off campus, and coached daily practices with his focus being on skills development of post players.

Prior to his time with the Hoosiers, Steele served as an assistant men's basketball coach at Wabash Valley College. Joining the Warriors in October, 2005, Steele also functioned as the program's Recruiting Coordinator and developed a skill instruction program. Steele had also spent a year with the Ohio State basketball program, serving as a graduate manager. His responsibilities included assisting with the skill instruction program and scouting of opposing teams, and also helped organize recruiting efforts.

So, not only had Steele put together a proven track record as a floor coach, his time spent working with AAU programs meant he was going to be an asset on the recruiting trail as well.

From 2001-06, Steele served as a coach for the Spiece/Indiana Adidas Elite AAU Basketball program. Recruiting high school players, he also coordinated practice and communicated plans to staff while organizing all travel and scheduling. Steele also served as assistant varsity basketball coach at Ben Davis High School while attending Butler University from 2001-2004.

Mack's second assistant, Brian Thornton, was a former standout player at Xavier that was able to bring a sense of familiarity with him of how things are done at Xavier when he was named Mack's second assistant coach.

"BT is a perfect fit for our staff," said Mack. "He's so well rounded that I believe he can really be someone our players can look up to; he was a First Team All-Atlantic 10 selection during his playing time here, he was also an All-Academic performer, so as a student-athlete, he was the total package. Brian is sharp, personable and eager to begin what I believe will be a long, successful coaching career at the college level."

One of things that will never be forgotten about Thornton is that he excelled both on and off the court at Xavier University. His senior season he was Xavier's first basketball student-athlete to earn Academic All-American honors. Thornton played two seasons at Xavier under Sean Miller after transferring from Vanderbilt University. Thornton led the team in scoring, rebounding, field goal percentage, and blocks before seeing his career end during a game against La Salle at Cintas Center in February of 2006.

Mario Mercurio had spent the past five years as Xavier University's first-ever Director of Basketball Administration under head coach Sean Miller. Additionally, Mercurio spent three years working with Thad Matta's staff, and another two years under the late former head coach Skip Prosser. Mercurio's responsibilities included non-conference scheduling, coordination of all team travel, and budget administrator. Signing high major neutral court games has also been an important part of the XU scheduling philosophy. Since taking over scheduling with former Xavier head coach Sean Miller in 2004, Xavier has added home-and-home series with Florida, Gonzaga, Virginia, LSU, Kansas State, Arizona State, Butler and Auburn.

Mack has always spoke highly of Mercurio, "I have said it count-less times, I think Mario is the best in the country at what he does, and there wasn't a moment's hesitation to keep him on board."

Lastly, Mack went outside the program and welcomed Orlando "Bino" Ranson to the staff. Ranson had previous stints on staffs at James Madison, Marist and Loyola of Maryland before Mack came calling. "Bino is a winner," said Mack, "He won as a player. He won as a coach. He's started programs from the ground up in his home-town of Baltimore. He's a star on the recruiting trail and will bring that winning mentality to the gym on an everyday basis."

When the staff was finalized Mack outlined what the responsi-bilities each member would have. Kelsey was slotted as Associate Head Coach, so he was there to assume the position of Head Coach when Mack was not available. During practice, Kelsey would mainly be spent advancing the development of the big men on the post.

Secondly, Kelsey was also responsible for being the lead recruiter in certain geographic areas and advance scouting during the sea-son. During games Kelsey would serve as the "defensive voice" on the floor, and lastly, would be involved in the oversight of numer-ous camps.

Travis Steele would also be heavily involved in recruiting, and same as Kelsey, would be responsible for monitoring a certain geo-graphical area that would include three classes worth of talent. Dur-ing games Steele would be the "offensive voice" for players on the floor, and was in charge of running warm ups and other facets of game day routine. During practice Steele was to oversee the development of guards in addition to evaluating all of the transcripts of each prospect Xavier was recruiting.

Bino Ranson was to assist in recruiting, perform advance scouting for a handful of opposing teams and monitor study hall throughout the year.

Mario Mercurio, Director of Basketball Administration, would continue to have a long list of duties; travel arrangements, oversight of the budget, working on future scheduling with Mack, preparation for official/unofficial visits, and coordination of distribution of away and home game tickets.

Brian Thornton, Director of Basketball Operations, had the primary duty of being the academic liaison to Sister Fleming. Fleming had become a living legend at Xavier.

She had become an advisor to the team back in 1985 when looking for opportunities beyond her law and accounting degrees. Fleming had been teaching on campus, but the chance to assist players on the team was a unique opportunity. Fleming is now a fixture within the program, greeting the players as they file into the locker room after every game. The players are quite aware of her presence and always treat her with the utmost respect.

Thornton was also charged with overseeing the organization of all Xavier Day Camps, Pell Grants, and was to be the point man for all communication with potential walk-ons. Thornton would also serve as the initial contact for all outside entities that wanted to attend practice/skill instruction and was to be the director for all player community service. Lastly, Thornton would compile and disseminate the weekly schedule to all staff members.

In addition to the primary coaching staff there are also additional members of the program that are an everyday part of the process who also have a long list of duties to attend to. That list included; Matt Jennings – Strength and Conditioning Coach, Justin Faris – Video Coordinator, and Steve Struble/Jeremy Growe – Program Assistants.

With the staff in place Mack was able to sharpen his focus on two remaining areas; demonstrating to the current players that there was stability within the program in spite of Miller's leaving. Mack wanted to assure the team, especially the upperclassmen, that their lives were not going to look a whole lot different than previous years.

Mack's second area of focus was to stay on top of recruiting. There were a number of players out there that Xavier had already been recruiting, including a verbal commitment from Jordan Latham from the Baltimore area. Mack's aim with Latham was to reaffirm that the Xavier he had committed to was still there, and that the staff was looking forward to Latham's joining the program.

As Mack set out to accomplish those two tasks, he soon learned that Derrick Brown had indeed chosen to go into the NBA draft in June. Knowing Brown's final decision made the task of evaluating current player personnel and deciding what roles certain players would fill a bit easier, but there was no question that Brown would be greatly missed, "We will certainly miss Derrick's enthusiasm, leadership, and production on the court, but I wish him nothing but the best as he and his family experience this exciting time in his life," said Mack.

The 2009-2010 Xavier team would be comprised of one senior and a number of players that had yet to get a lot of floor time. On the other hand, it was also going to be a team that had a number of players that had tasted a bit of postseason success which was an invaluable experience for players to have at any level. Overall, it was a very talented group that had the potential to do special things.

That superior talent began with sophomore Brad Redford who had been ranked by FOXSports.com as the second-best shooter in college basketball for 2009-10 on its list of the top 50 shooters. Mack agreed, "I've never coached a better shooter than Brad Redford." Redford led the Atlantic 10 Conference the year before in three-point percentage at 46.5 percent. That established a new school record at Xavier, which broke the mark of .437 set at Xavier by then-senior Jamie Gladden during the 1992-93 season. What made the accomplishment all the more impressive was the fact that a large portion of Redford's attempts came from way beyond the new and deeper three point line. A Xavier crowd favorite with his deep-range bombs, Redford's 53 three-pointers marked the third-highest total for a freshman in Xavier history behind Stanley Burrell's 61 in 2004-05, and Xavier freshman record holder Romain Sato who threw in 65 in 2000-01.

While Redford was going to be lethal beyond the arc, it meant that many teams will be defending him that far away from the basket a little tougher each year. Because of that, Mack stressed to Redford, "that he really has to work harder on penetrating the defense with the ball and moving more around the floor to create open shots. If Brad can continue to progress in this area it will then make him a threat to score from multiple places on the floor."

Even though fellow guard Jordan Crawford received more ink coming into the new season, Mark Lyons was poised to make a huge impact after sitting out last season as a freshman. Mack said, "He's a big-time athlete that can put pressure on the opposing defense with his speed, and is fearless.

"Cheeks' ability to get the ball up the floor and knock down free throws will be a huge help to us throughout the season, I know he is looking forward to the challenge of being such an integral part of the team this year."

Center Kenny Frease led the team in blocked shots at 1.26 per game, which put him 10th in the conference a year earlier. Frease notched a career-high five blocks in the Pittsburgh game in the NCAA Tournament East Regional Semifinal the year before.

"Kenny needs to continue putting forth the effort to get better in all facets of the game. Since we will be a team that gets up and down the floor a bit quicker this year he is going to have to be prepared and in tip top shape, ready to contribute, because we are counting on him to deliver at both ends of the floor."

Jordan Crawford, a transfer from Indiana University who had sat out the previous year, was generating quite a buzz nationally for the YouTube highlight of him dunking over LeBron James earlier in the summer.

Even though the film clip was impressive it paled in comparison to the other parts of the all-around game that Crawford was going to put in display all season long. "Not really sure where to begin with Jordan, he is an explosive talent that has that rare ability to just take a game over at any given moment. There is no question he will be the catalyst for our offense this year. Like many players though, Jordan needs to continue to improve defensively and be smart with shot selection."

Jason Love had started at center for Xavier 56 times in the last two seasons, including all 35 the past year. Love was the only senior on this year's team, and also the top returning scorer and rebounder.

Love had recorded an 82-24 (.773) record during his first three seasons, and was 21 wins shy of the school record of 103 set by former teammate B.J. Raymond, heading into the season.

Love already shared the Xavier record for most career NCAA Tournament wins (six) with Raymond and 2009 XU graduate Derrick Brown. "I'm not sure if I have ever seen anyone work as hard as Jason Love in my career. When he was a freshman he came in here and weighed 286 pounds and had 24% body fat. Entering his final year in a Xavier uniform Love had transformed his body to a leaner 245 pounds with 9.3% body fat."

Even though Love was soft spoken both on and off the floor there was no question among those in the clubhouse who the leader was on the team, "Jason leads by example at everything, I know he is going to have a great season. I'm gonna hate to see him go, but I'm excited for his future because he is going to be a success no matter what he does."

One of two returning starters along with Jason Love, Dante Jackson was named to the 2009-10 pre-season Atlantic 10 Conference All-Defensive Team along with Love.

Over his first two years Jackson had developed the reputation as a big game player, as evidenced by his performance in the 2009 NCAA Tournament where he averaged 10.0 points, 2.7 rebounds, 2.0 assists and 2.3 steals for in Xavier's three tournament games.

Jackson made one of the biggest shots of his young career in the NCAA Tournament when he nailed a three-pointer against Georgia that put Xavier ahead for good at 52-49 with 7:21 left. Xavier, who had trailed by 11 points with 16 minutes left, led the rest of the way after his shot and the shot was nominated for a Pontiac "Game Changing Performance" Jackson's versatility showed as he started the last 11 games at point guard, averaging 7.8 points, 4.0 rebounds, 2.7 assists and a 2.73-to-1.00 assist-to-turnover ratio for those starts.

"Dante can do so many different things for you on the floor which can make him hard to defend at times, but it's what he does at the defensive end where he really shines. His ability to defend on and off the ball is flawless. He understands our defensive schemes inside and out."

Sophomore guard Terrell Holloway started 13 games as a freshman where he had an impact on the floor at the free throw line and controlling the ball. Mack said of Holloway, "He will do so many things for us this year throughout the game. He gives us an experienced ball handler to get the ball up the floor when we get pressured and is almost even money from the free throw line.

"There was nobody that worked harder this summer to prepare for the upcoming season than Terrell. Our players implemented something called the 'Gun Club' to measure how many shots they took in the off season. Nobody ever came close to the number of shots that Terrell took. It will be fun to see that hard work pay off for him this season."

Jamel McLean, a junior that had transferred to Xavier after his freshman year at Tulsa, was expected to get a lot of floor time and contribute heavily. McLean played a larger role down the stretch the previous season grabbing six rebounds in a first round NCAA Tournament win over Portland State. In Xavier's second round game against Wisconsin, McLean hauled down four rebounds and slammed home three dunks for six points that propelled Xavier into the Sweet 16 for the second year in a row. Mack was also counting on the development of other players like Andrew Taylor, Brian Walsh, and Jeff Robinson. Their progress could provide some added depth off the bench.

Even though summer had arrived Mack still had a lot on his plate. June was a month that would fill up with "unofficial visits" to campus, Mack's own Summer Camp, an elite camp for prospects on Xavier's radar, and an annual high school team camp.

July is perhaps the hardest month of the year from a travel standpoint. Every year the 6th through the 15th and the 22nd through the 31st are dates that are open for on-the-road recruiting. July is also when many of the AAU tournaments are held including the national events in Las Vegas and at Disney World. Mack said of the schedule, "These events are part of the job. You have to have a presence there each and every day of the recruiting period because kids take note of which programs are watching them."

August is a bit of a respite before school starts up again in the latter weeks of the month. The first day of classes was when Mack and the other coaches were able to start working with the team again. "The first thing we needed to do when the kids got back was assess where they were from a conditioning perspective."

Mack had the team do nothing but lift weights for the first three days, and on the first weekend had the team travel out to Mack's old high school, St. Xavier, for their traditional one-mile run. Each position had a time they had to beat; for the guards it was 5:25, wings/forwards was 5:40, and big men/posts was 6:00.

If a player was able to beat his position time it meant no conditioning for two weeks, those who unfortunately did not beat their time had conditioning at 7 a.m. five days a week for the next two weeks.

6 of 12 made their time, "which was disappointing, but not deflating. I certainly expected those that didn't make their time to get their butts in shape because before they know it, the first day of practice will be here."

A few days before practice began; the coaching staff administered the dreaded "Riley Test." The drill, created by former NBA coaching legend Pat Riley, consists of a series of 10 sprints that players run from baseline to baseline. There are six series in all in which the player has to finish in a certain amount of time depending on their position. They get 2.5 minutes to rest and they step back on that line and run another 10.

Mack said of the drill, "We run six 10's. Players don't have to always be under a certain time, but they do have to achieve a pre-determined average time for their six sets of sprints. So if they run that first one really hard and put some seconds in the bank, they can maybe run the fifth and sixth ones a little bit slower. There's a little bit of smarts to it. I know our guys hate it, but it really shows us where we are conditioning-wise, and how we stand individually regarding mental toughness."

Ten of twelve players passed.

It was a big deal in the minds of the players to have that milestone behind them; for one, they are glad for it to be over with, and secondly it gives them confidence to let them know they are ready for practice.

Six months after being hired, an eager Chris Mack watched as his team took to the practice floor for the first time under his tenure,

"You don't really have time to stop and think about the moment because you are so focused on what lies ahead of you. It just felt good to finally get going, like the starting gates had opened and we could begin running.

"I would like to think that the intensity that our players are used to performing at in practice will be there," Mack said, "I'd like to think that although there are a few different voices in the gym, we're still going to be doing what we do. Jason Love needs to be more vocal as a leader and share the knowledge he has amassed defensively and offensively to our younger guys.

"We have a unique situation here; none of our returners averaged double-figures in scoring, Jason has logged some minutes and he has to lead by example for the other players on the team to learn quickly. Unlike some years in the past, we are deep at the guard position, and increased speed will provide more versatility at both ends of the floor."

Mack spoke at length on what he wanted to accomplish within the first few weeks of practice leading up to the first exhibition game against Rollins College, "I'm looking forward to building toward the first exhibition game and seeing how far we can come together as a team. Our expectations at Xavier haven't changed. We want to compete for the conference championship every year and play in the postseason - the NCAA Tournament - and advance. We'll do what we can to work toward that in the preseason.

"I view the first couple weeks of practice as a real coming together for our players. Like any coach at this time of year, you always feel like you've got a long way to go. But we'll get there. I love our talent level and I love our competitiveness amongst the team."

The next big date on the calendar was Saturday October 24th. This was the date of "Musketeer Madness" which would be the first time the players got to play in front of a crowd.

"Our guys and our staff were excited about Musketeer Madness on Saturday. It was a break from the regular practice routine. We practiced early in the day to get our work done. Musketeer Madness is for our fans, players and families to enjoy themselves. It's always a great atmosphere and a good chance for our guys to get used to playing in front of a crowd."

"We invited a lot of the basketball alums, including a lot of my former teammates, to join us Saturday. We got together for a little reception beforehand. The stories brought a lot of laughs. They always do," said Mack of the day's events.

The following week it was back to work. Even though the daily practice routine may seem as though it would get monotonous Mack saw it differently, "It's satisfying when you watch the DVD of practice each night and you can clearly see the progress."

As would be the theme for most of the upcoming season, defense was the priority. Mack explained, "Defense is always the priority. We demand effort on every single possession. We have also been working a lot on communication. We need guys to be more vocal if we are to become the type of defensive team I want us to be. It's not in the nature of some guys to be vocal, but players need to speak up for the defense to be effective. We are making progress in this area, but we still have work to do.

"A good example is for big guys like Kenny (Frease) and Jason (Love) to realize that they have an advantage with the communication on defense because as post players they see the entire floor. They are now in a position, especially Jason, to get more vocal on the floor because often times good defense is based on out-loud communication."

Defensive tenets are drilled into the players head's repeatedly during countless practice drills. Assistant Coach Kelsey spent a lot of time at the beginning of the year going over "gap awareness." Gaps are the areas that fall between each player on the court, and Kelsey wanted the players to learn to not only concentrate on who they were responsible for guarding, but also to keep an eye on what is happening in the gaps closest to you.

"You have to have a strong gap awareness, know what is going on around you, it's the foundation of our defensive philosophy, crowd the court, make it tough for the opponent to move the ball around," Kelsey would instruct.

Mack would quickly move the team from one drill to the next at a breakneck pace with each drill timing out at 24 seconds on the game clock. "We always want things to move faster in practice, hence the short time clock, if they can think at this pace they should be able to handle the adrenaline that comes with game time situations."

One of the toughest drills run at almost every practice was 85 in 2. The team would split up evenly at each end of the court. At the sound of the whistle the players would run down each side of the court passing the ball back and forth with coaches and managers until finally laying the ball into the basket at the other end. The goal was to make 85 baskets in two minutes which the team often would accomplish, but not by much.

A week before the Rollins game, Mack was getting frustrated with some sloppy play during a handful of decent drills when he blew his whistle to stop practice and shouted, "You know what, we sure will miss Derrik Brown, someone who had a complete understanding of what we were trying to do on defense. You have to pay attention on what is going on away from the ball at all times."

A few minutes later Mack remained dissatisfied and sent the team to the end line to run, "Fellas, I don't need to see this garbage, get on the line. Guys we can run all night, we can come back again like last night, now let's go!"

Last night had seen the team called back to practice in the late evening in an attempt to send a message that everyone needed to get their act together. Mack said, "They better get it together, and quick, uniform time is right around the corner, then it's for real. Thinking back to when I played, as players we always felt ready after about four practices. No doubt, coaches and players think differently. Rollins College will give everyone in the program a sense of where we are and where we need to go."

Even though Mack showed a lot of frustration about the team's attentiveness in the early going, overall, behind the scenes, he was pleased, "The preseason practices have been competitive, lasting around two hours a day and with a purpose. That approach has been consistent at Xavier since I returned six years ago. Keeping our guys energized both mentally and physically is crucial for us in March. This year is no different. Winning championships isn't about polls. It's about consistency and bringing great play and effort to practice in every drill every day. Champions are consistent every practice. The preseason practices are very important to setting the tone for this season."

Mack was very pleased with the progress of one player in particular, not just for his effort in practice, but for the personal hardship that he was dealing with off the court, "Jamel McLean has really stood out. Last year, he had a tendency to drift mentally and consequently had some games where he was virtually a non-factor. He's worked hard to change that perception.

"Sadly, though he was dealt a crushing blow recently when his father passed away suddenly. He's been gone for a few days, but will soon rejoin us for practice. One thing he knows through this tragedy is that he has a family of players, coaches and managers that are here for him."

At the team's next practice Mack had the team gather around at mid court before starting, "Fellas we only have one day until our first pre-season test against Rollins. I want you to give me a good, solid hour, hour and a half today working hard on pressuring the ball. Remember it's 'Do what we do' around here, so let's go."

Mack spent time with the big men showing them how he wanted them to move their feet to wall up the offensive player while keeping their hands up high at all times, "Rollins has a bunch of guys that can't jump, so don't make it easy on them by leaving your feet, stay grounded with high hands."

Mack also wanted to see more toughness when the team set screens away from the ball, "Guys don't get soft on screens; stop, plant your feet, and, boom, hit the other guy hard. Start wearing them down from the outset, be physical early."

The next evening saw Chris Mack take the floor for the first time as Head Coach in a game at Cintas Center. "You know, I was so intent on making sure we stayed focused on what the team needed to do to beat Rollins, I never really gave much thought to the overall meaning of the evening for me."

The game was never really in doubt. Xavier won 86-47. Mack said afterward, "I was pretty pleased with what we saw overall, no real surprises, and no real concerns. What is mainly left between now and the beginning of the season is to keep the team focused. We don't want [the team] riding highs and lows from game to game, just continue to work on the principles of defense – ball screens and interior screens with lots of film afterwards."

Later in the week Xavier welcomed Northern Kentucky to the Cintas Center and handed them a similar beat-down to the one administered to Rollins College to win 83-66. Mack was using the game as a chance to run a few new offensive sets, see where the team needed to improve on defense, and generally get everyone into the game to see how they handled the situation, "Overall it was fine, they got a bit sloppy at times. We could have been better on both sides of the ball. We need to move better without the ball and be more aggressive on rebounding, which we will work on starting today."

With two exhibition games and several preseason practices in the books, some of the players started to get a bit cagey as the opener neared, forcing Mack to take tighter control of the reigns down the stretch. Mack had the team running a number of drills that were pretty rough on the defensive side of the ball in practice. After a short while the players were talking it up to each other and complaining about a call, with freshman Mark Lyons being the most vocal.

Mack yelled, "Cheeks I'm done listening to you complain, you do it again, you're gone. I'll stop it right now and put you on the line and we'll run if you want. It's your choice." A short time later the players were able to take a break and shoot free throws. That was when Mack pulled Lyons aside to talk with him, "Cheeks your attitude is setting the wrong tone for the whole team. Get it together, people are watching you."

Cheeks replied, "I will coach."

Mack later said, "With Cheeks he is very competitive which sometimes makes him tough to coach. He gets wrapped up in the competition, but he still needs to listen. You have to roll with it, and know when to jump him."

When the team hit the showers Mack looked over some notes he had made on the practice drill sheet that he has in his back pocket at every practice. It appeared that the beginning of the season was starting to weigh on his every thought, "We need to keep pushing them to get better. I like what I'm seeing, but as soon as you let them know that, there can be a tendency to let up, and we can't allow that."

November 11th was certainly not another normal day on Chris Mack's calendar. That day, the second Tuesday in November, is what is known as Signing Day, a day when high school seniors around the nation can sign their letter of intent that locks them in to where they will be going to school the next fall.

Xavier was fortunate to land four outstanding seniors for their incoming freshman class in 2010, national letters of intent from young men who will be a part of the Xavier team beginning with the 2010-11 season, an impressive list of signees which earned Xavier a top 20 recruiting class ranking by rivals.com and many other experts.

The signees included Jay Canty, a 6-5, 185-pound guard/forward from Oak Ridge (NC) Military Academy; Jordan Latham, a 6-8, 220-pound forward from City College High School in Baltimore, Md.; Justin Martin, a 6-7, 200-pound forward from Mountain State Academy in Beckley, W.Va.; and Griffin McKenzie, a 6-9, 220-pound forward from Cincinnati's Moeller High School.

Mack was excited about the signing of Canty: "Jay is a terrific player and an even better young man. He could be a dominant rebounder and defender in our system as well."

Jordan Latham, ranked 121st by rivals.com, averaged 12 points, seven rebounds and five blocks a game last season. Mack said it wasn't easy, but over time Latham decided on Xavier, "After committing to the previous staff, Jordan decided to open up his recruitment during the period of time in which there was not a head coach in place. Ultimately though, Jordan felt that there wasn't a better fit in the country than Xavier for both his academic and basketball future. Jordan has the size, quickness and toughness to cement his place here."

Justin Martin, ranked 83rd by rivals.com, averaged 10.4 ppg as a junior at Lawrence North High School in Indianapolis, IN, the same school that sent Xavier current freshman Jeff Robinson. Mack said Martin can really shoot the ball, "Justin has a high IQ for the game, can shoot it from deep and is just beginning to scratch the surface of his potential as a player. Justin is more than a shooter. He can really pass and has the ability to rebound defensively and push the ball."

Griffin McKenzie, ranked 115th by rivals.com, averaged 9.4 points and 3.8 rebounds a game as a junior at Cincinnati Moeller, although his production was slowed last season by an injury. The prognosis for the upcoming season was that McKenzie was going to be 100% healthy, and was expected to lead his team to great success.

Mack was excited that another local standout, McKenzie, would be a Musketeer, "Griffin was as sought after as any skilled post player in the country during the all-important month of July. He'll be considered a weapon at the college level, and should continue the lineage of great players from my old high school conference, the Greater Cincinnati League."

Mack spent much of the day fulfilling media requests to comment on the signings, but was thinking about Youngstown State and opening night in the back of his mind the whole time. Mack seemed ready to break into a sprint down to the practice floor when it was time, "It's an exciting day for the program every year. We got four solid players that will contribute to the team immediately next year. Overall, it was a good year recruiting, we didn't really feel like we lost out on anyone we were dying to get."

Later that afternoon, before practice Mack pulled the team together in the locker room to go over some of the personnel from Youngstown State and watch some of their offensive sets on film.

Again, the focus was going to be on how to defend the other team, "that's how we win games, we'll score enough points, I don't worry about that, we just need to make sure we take care of business on the defensive end of the floor."

Mack did most of the talking while the film ran, "All right let's talk game plan. Youngstown State likes to move without the ball a bunch so our big guys need to be helpers while the smalls are chasing. YSU has a movement where they will hand off or set a ball screen up top. If you see the forward taking big steps into this screen it usually means they are getting a hand off, so look for that during those times."

Mack ran this play a number of times to reiterate the point.

"Post men, you will need to give help off the ball, be aware of what is going on around you. Look for their guards to dribble drive a lot, but they will never finish, they usually hand off."

Again, Mack ran the play multiple times on the screen for emphasis.

"Lastly, remember to talk, talk, talk. They rely on their guards to score, a large percent of scoring comes from their three seniors. In order to win you must shut them down."

When the film session was over Mack took a minute to read an email to the team that he had received earlier in the week which had given praise to the team on how organized and attentive they were during the National Anthem of the first two preseason games, "I read this email as a reminder to you to remember that people are watching your every move. It's up to you to represent yourself and the University the right way at all times. I want you to remember that when the season gets underway."

Later, as the final practice before the regular season started to wind down Mack confidently said, "I think they are ready. Today's practice was upbeat and loose which is a good sign. I know that in the coming year we are going to miss the leadership of the three seniors that left; B.J. Raymond, Derrick Brown and C.J. Anderson. They were a significant part of our success over the past four years, and it will be hard to look out on the floor and not see them suited up. Their legacy is one lined with championships and success. Our guys now are much younger and need to model their preparation, their practice habits and their determination after those three."

Sitting at the edge of the scorer's table with his arms folded, Mack looked at his players as they filed off the floor towards the locker room and smiled, "So far, so good, I like what I'm seeing. I think we're gonna have a whole lot of fun this year."

Chapter 3

Here We Go

"Fellas this is it. This is the beginning of the NCAA basketball season. At some point tonight you are going to realize why you put in all of the hard work from this summer and fall," Mack said as he addressed the team before heading out to the floor.

All last minute instructions had been given on Youngstown State and their personnel, and it was now time to take the floor to either become 1-0 or 0-1. Now it was for real.

Mack was intensely focused as he and his assistants made their way through the tunnel from the locker room to the floor. Those close to Mack know that when the time is right a movie reference is sure to follow, and opening night of his college head coaching career was no different. Mack decided to go with a Gene Hackman quote from *Hoosiers* when he walked onto the floor and said to his assistants as he looked up at a capacity crowd of 10,250 in the Cintas Center, "Welcome to Indiana High School basketball."

The players had already entered into Cintas Center to thunderous applause and a home crowd that had high expectations not only for opening night, but the season as well.

The players on the other hand seemed very loose and confident when they had grouped together chanting "1 and 0, 1 and 0!" before taking the floor. After the national anthem and team introductions it was time for the opening tip. Mack took what would become his customary seat on the bench for the rest of the season, third down from the scorer's table with Pat Kelsey and Brian Thornton to his right, and Travis Steele and Bino Ranson to his left.

"By opening night I still had not gotten used to where I wanted to be on the sidelines yet. As an assistant I was so used to sitting I forgot that I was the one that needed to get up and do the yelling. I'm sure I'll settle into some sort of routine as the season goes on," said Mack.

Mack was calmly watching things, sipping from a bottle of water, when the ball was tossed into the air for the opening tip, which Xavier controlled. A little over a minute and a half later at the 18:24 mark, Terrell Holloway sank a shot from the left wing and the first points of the season were on the board. Xavier was solid from the outset, racing out to an 8-0 lead which ballooned to 13-2. At the half Xavier held a 24-point lead which left Mack with little to say to the team during the break, "We talked a little bit about continuing to have an aggressive attitude in the second half, don't let up. We also got burned on a few in-bounds plays under our own basket, so we talked about making adjustments in the second half."

The second half was identical to the first; Xavier led comfortably, then finally closed things out with a convincing win 83-57. Jordan Crawford led five Musketeers in double-figure scoring with 14 points. Jason Love and Mark Lyons each scored 12 points, Brad Redford scored 11 points, and Terrell Holloway chipped in 10 points. Elsewhere, Love grabbed 8 rebounds, and Holloway and Lyons each had 3 assists. Xavier had now won 20 straight regular season openers and extended its winning streak at Cintas Center to 10 games.

Xavier was consistent from the field shooting 51 percent, and going 30-37 from the charity stripe. Xavier edged out the Penguins in the battle of the boards by a count of 39-to-31. The Musketeers excelled in post play scoring 28 points in the paint as opposed to Youngstown's 18 points in the paint.

Mack said afterward, "Well, it's good to get game one under our belt. Fortunately our guys came out from the get-go and defended like I've asked them to in practice. In the second half I thought we played the score a little bit. We've got to correct that. We move forward to Tuesday night against Bowling Green."

Even though many wanted to talk about the victory being Mack's first as head coach, he wanted none of it, "I feel like I've had many wins at

Xavier, whether as a player or as an assistant coach. It's not about me."

When the team finally assembled in the locker room after the game Mack went to the dry erase board and wrote the schedule for tomorrow that would include practice in the morning. After complete silence filled the air Mack said with a smile, "lighten up, I was joking." After a collective sigh and a few laughs the team listened to Mack's assessment of the game, "Great job tonight guys, you did everything that was asked of you during practice. Real pleased with how well we shot from the line. In the second half we started playing the score and we can't fall into that trap. We can't ever stop competing.

"Overall, though, good win tonight. Enjoy this one, but also be smart about what you do and with whom. In a few days we will take on Bowling Green, a team that is much bigger than Youngstown State, one that will play a lot of zone compared to man to man so we need to be ready to come back and get prepared."

Mack closed with this final thought, "Gentlemen, welcome to the college basketball season, now it's for real, St. Joe's won tonight-they are 1 and 0, Richmond 1 and 0, UMass 0 and 1, they lost to Central Florida. Every game counts, let's stay focused!"

Even though the team's work for the night was over, Mack still had a ways to go. There was the gauntlet of local radio, Fox TV, and a press conference yet to be had. An hour or so later, Mack's work was done. After a long day, the first of many to come, Mack jokingly wondered aloud as he left the arena that, "If I retired now I would be the only undefeated coach in the history of Xavier. I might want to consider that."

Based on the wry smile Mack showed as he disappeared out the back door it was obvious this was not going to be the case. His mind was already focused on beating Bowling Green.

Time goes quickly in college basketball, three days had passed and it was game day again. Mack had some concerns about the adjustments his players needed to make from their first game, "Bowling Green will play a lot of zone, some man, but majority of the time a 2/3 zone. We want to move the ball around the perimeter against their zone, get the ball inside, keep good size on the back of the zone, and make their guards work on the top side.

"I want to move Brad Redford around so they have to account for him, he will stretch the zone. We can steal some points in transition before they even set up."

On and on it goes; the litany of a Division I coach, always thinking a few plays ahead. For Mack and his program though, the opponents may change but the approach does not, "Even though our opponents will throw different things at us, we still want to keep it simple for the kids, we are not going to change game to game; we are a man to man team on defense, and we like to move the ball quickly and score in transition regardless of who we play. Now don't get me wrong, if you run into a team that is good enough to take some of those things away from you, you have to adapt quickly, and we certainly have the personnel to carry out plan b if need be."

Louis Orr, the head coach at Bowling Green, and Mack had some prior history since Orr served as an assistant when Mack played at Xavier. The two shared a warm embrace near midcourt before player introductions. Mack spoke highly of Orr, "Louis Orr is as good a person as there is in college basketball. He was so good to me when I was at Xavier. He really knew how to capture a player's attention. As a long time NBA player, he had all the tricks of the trade. He was eager to share what he knew, and I was lucky that he was around our program when I played at Xavier."

Bowling Green made the first basket of the game giving Xavier their first deficit of the year, but that was quickly erased as Bowling Green elected to stay in a zone defense that Xavier's Brad Redford shredded from beyond the three point line.

Even though he was shining on the offensive side of the floor Mack stayed on Redford for his effort defensively, "Brad you have got to chase your man, stay on him, your man is getting too many looks."

It was a theme that Mack had stressed with Redford from the preseason on, "Brad has to continue to work hard at defending the ball and getting himself open more on the offensive end of the floor. Those two areas will be key to defining Brad's success all year."

At halftime Xavier held a commanding lead, 51-28. There was not much that Mack and the staff had seen that needed immediate attention in the second half. If the team continued with the current effort Mack knew they would walk away with a win.

When Mack came in to address the team you would have thought the game was tied. In a loud tone Mack stressed the importance of working through screens and defending the ball, "We gave up 6 points on blast cuts. You need to see your man and the ball! Good players see both when the ball goes inside!"

Mack then wrote Duke, North Carolina, and Kansas on the dry erase board, "Fellas when I see these teams scroll along the bottom of ESPN and see a halftime score of 51-28 I can tell you what the final is going to be. These teams have a killer instinct, I've seen it up close, they want to kill your spirit in the 2nd half, but not on offense-on defense. The offense will take care of itself. Do the same tonight to Bowling Green, make them quit, we ended on a 22-3 run, let's come out strong and end this thing, let's go!"

The team collectively got the message and with runs of 22-3 and 30-4 Xavier pounded Bowling Green throughout the second half and pulled away for a comfortable win 101-57.

Jordan Crawford led all scorers for the second game in a row and was joined in double-figures by Brad Redford, Jason Love and Terrell Holloway who each scored 12 points. Xavier dominated in all facets of the game, out-rebounding the Falcons 43-to-26 and holding a 13-to-2 edge in second chance points. Xavier also kept up an early-season trend of winning the fast break points battle 23-to-6.

Obviously pleased with the overall performance from the whole team Mack spoke afterward about the effort of Jordan Crawford, "I want to challenge Jordan [Crawford] to be as good on the defensive end as he is on the offensive end. If he can do it, the sky is the limit. He made quite an improvement from game one to game two."

Senior Jason Love merited some praise from the head coach also, "I thought Jason [Love] did a great job. I've said it a million times; he's the consummate professional. I was really happy for him tonight."

Following the team prayer in the locker room Mack told his players that tonight was a tremendous all-around effort, "Both halves were a mirror image of each other. If we can commit on defense and continue to develop good habits, trust me, as your coach, we can do some special things during the remainder of the year.

"Enjoy tonight, be smart in your comments to the press and where you spend your time with family and friends. Next up is Sacred Heart, they will be bigger and faster than Bowling Green, they have three guards that can score and run, so enjoy this one, but be ready to get prepared starting tomorrow."

After the game, Mack, his wife Christi, Rivals.com writer Brian Snow, and Scout.com writer Evan Daniels made their way out of Cintas Center heading down I-471 to Longneck's Sports Bar in Wilder, Kentucky. Mack had frequented Longneck's over the years as an assistant after games, and this year, despite Mack's role as head coach, that would not change. After so many hours of preparing for a game through practice, film, and meetings, relaxing with friends immediately after the game helped Mack enjoy the grueling demands of coaching at the Division I level.

One would have thought Xavier had yet to win a game based on the intensity of the next few practices. Mack doubled the pace of practice to make sure that his team was not getting lazy early in the season. Mack often would interrupt practice to make a point. On rebounding, "Our box out percentages are terrible, our opponents average near 12 per game, let's get to the ball!" On turnovers, "Too many turnovers fellas, you have to hold onto the ball. Redford, you just got stripped by Lyons using his pinky finger. C'mon, be strong with the ball!"

Later, when Sacred Heart rolled into town, it seemed as though the pedal to the floor approach worked. For the second consecutive game, Jordan Crawford established a new career high when he scored 26 points to lead Xavier in the win 105-65. Put simply, Crawford's performance bordered on unconscious, 11-of-15 from the floor, including a 4-of-5 effort from beyond the 3-point arc.

Senior center Jason Love added his second straight double-double with a 14-point, 15-rebound effort. He was 5-of-8 from the floor and a perfect 4-for-4 from the free throw line. Love's 15 rebounds marked the first time a Musketeer has hauled in 15 or more boards since former Musketeer Derrick Brown turned the trick against BYU in the first round of the 2007 NCAA Tournament.

Freshman guard Mark Lyons tied a career high with 12 points and established a new career best with four assists. Lyons was a solid 8-of-10 from the free throw line. Sophomore center Kenny Frease scored 14 points on 6-of-9 shooting. Junior forward Jamel McLean scored eight points on 3-of-4 shooting and snared a career-high 13 rebounds.

Sacred Heart trailed by three points, 9-6, in the early goings of the first half but the Musketeers stepped squarely on the Pioneers' throat with a 25-6 run over an 8:15 stretch and jumped out to a commanding 36-12 lead with 6:45 remaining in the first half.

The Musketeers would never let up and extended their lead to as many as 48 points en route to the 105-65 win. Xavier continued to shoot well on the offensive end of the floor, 56.7 percent, but more impressive to Mack was the effort on the defensive end that helped the Pioneers to just 34.4 percent from the floor, "I was pleased with our performance tonight. We came out with a lot of energy. When you play a team that shoots the ball as well from the three point line as Sacred Heart, you get a little nervous. I thought Dante [Jackson] was great early. I felt like our team took a step forward in assist to turnover ratio [22 assists, 9 turnovers]. I told my guys in the locker room, spring training is over. Tough games are ahead."

Mack continued to be pleased with the role that Jason Love was stepping into, "Jason Love has always been capable. He worked hard during the off season. It's more than just being in the right place at the right time. As well as he seals his man, he can be a terror on the offensive glass."

The first three games served their purpose; to serve as a warm up to the next handful of games on the schedule. The team was faced with a road trip to the Old Spice Classic in Orlando over Thanksgiving weekend which was going to provide a solid early season test against arguably the best talent Xavier had faced. After the trip down south, two huge games loomed; Cincinnati at home for the Crosstown Shootout and Butler on the road at Hinkle Fieldhouse.

The team appeared loose in their last practice before the Old Spice Classic. Brad Redford was hassled by others while continuing to make a ridiculous number of three-pointers in a row that left center Kenny Frease shaking his head in amazement. Mack, meanwhile, was at the other end of the floor conducting individual meetings with Terrell Holloway and Dante Jackson to further stress some points brought up during film sessions earlier in the day.

Mack then gathered the team at midcourt for a quick message, "Fellas, last year when we went to Puerto Rico for a similar event we got a lot of disrespect from ESPN and others about how we were on the lower side of the talent pool going in. We're not gonna listen to that again this year. If we remember to box out and play defense we can win down there. Let's play in the right game on Friday, not the consolation game. Give me an hour and a half with good energy, good leadership before we get out of town, then let's go have some fun."

The team quickly settled into the routine of another hard practice. Mack knew that his team was going to face their toughest challenge yet, "Marquette will pressure the ball more than anyone else we have played. We need to be ready for that. They are going to pick us up well away from the basket; we haven't seen that yet, so we need to get prepared." Mack believed that even though the ball pressure defense from Marquette was going to present some problems, he felt that Xavier's quickness might be able to get the game a bit more up tempo to offset being caught in just a half-court game.

The team finished with series of defensive drills on the post, working on getting their body into the man they were guarding while keeping their hands high in the air, hence the term high hands.

Mack can usually be heard yelling this order in from the sidelines, "I feel that if you have your hands up high for the ref to see he is less likely to call a foul on you, so we stress that to our players."

Even though the opponent was different, the drills sent the same message; pressure defense and stay attached on screens. It is this constant reminder of a consistent message that has led to Xavier success over the years.

"We don't want to change who we are for every different game. Our guys have grown up in a system here that focuses on a few fundamental areas that we preach religiously. That way nothing gets lost in delivering the message," said Mack walking off the court.

Two days later Jason Love posted a career high 21 points and 19 rebounds to lead Xavier in the tournament opener, but it was not enough; the program suffered its first loss of the year to Marquette 71-61.

Love started the game strong, scoring four points in the first three minutes which keyed a 7-1 Xavier run in the early going. Xavier led the first 13:45 of the game but Marquette rallied to take a 33-29 lead at the half thanks to a 13-7 run in the final six minutes of the first period.

Xavier regained the lead at the 17:17 mark on a layup by Love that gave the Musketeers a 37-36 lead. The two teams traded offensive blows for most of the second half until Marquette took the lead for good on a Maurice Acker shot at the 8:50 mark to put the score 51-49 in their favor.

Afterwards, Mack spoke candidly about his assessment of his Xavier's first loss of the year," We were favored going in; I think we played too confident and consequently we gambled a bit more than usual on defense. Offensively we took a number of bad shots. Marquette played hard, I thought we would handle the ball pressure, but didn't. They forced us so far out from the basket we couldn't get set and that rattled us."

Mack however was undaunted and positive moving forward, "As we get away from this we'll get better. We are disappointed that defensively we got away from what we do and tried too much. We really got on them later at the hotel stressing that tonight's effort defensively is not what we teach. We got into too many situations with our back to the ball and got caught sleeping. It has to change, and quick."

It certainly did in the next game against Creighton. Xavier never trailed while guard Jordan Crawford got things back to normal posting 22 points including 8-of-12 from the field and 4-of-5 from behind the arch that gave Xavier the 80-67 win.

"We were much more selective from the floor and it showed, we shot 53.7 percent from the field and 50 percent from the 3-point line," Mack said.

"It's always good when you can stop a losing streak at one. We came out with good intensity and dominated most of the game. It was good to see that bounce back mentality from our kids."

Xavier blew the game open at the 10:09 mark in the second half when junior forward Jamel McLean threw down a thunderous dunk to give Xavier 65-49 lead. McLean finished with six points and four rebounds on the day. Sophomore point guard Terrell Holloway was second on the team in scoring with 12.

Lastly, the message that was succinctly delivered to the team a few nights earlier back at the hotel regarding their defensive effort got through. Xavier won the battle of the boards with 33 rebounds to Creighton's 31 while also holding their opponent to just 38.8 percent shooting.

The next day, Xavier closed out the road trip with a loss to Baylor 69-64. Despite another solid performance from junior forward Jamel McLean that included 17 points and five rebounds, the loss put Xavier at 1-2 for the weekend and 4-2 overall.

Sophomore guard Jordan Crawford delivered another solid outing; with 16 points and six rebounds. Senior Jason Love led the Musketeers in rebounding with seven.

Baylor came out of the gate strong in the first half, going on an 11-2 run in the first three minutes of play. Six of the first 11 Baylor points came from senior guard Tweety Carter's three pointers. Carter finished the game with 27 points on 8-of-16 from the field and 6-of-10 from behind the arch.

"Today we lost to a good team with a player in Carter that just lit it up. We fought hard up until the end, but it wasn't enough. We'll use it as a learning experience," said Mack after the game.

Shortly after landing back home at Lunken Airport Mack tried to summarize the holiday trip, "I think we learned a lot this past weekend. I think we showed our youth a bit in some things we did at both ends of the floor. We can learn from that and get better moving forward. The games only get bigger from here and I believe that we learned some things down in Florida that will help us later in the year. You would like to win every game, you can't, but when you don't you need to take something from those games you lose and I think we will, but we'll continue to preach and teach our system."

The following Monday Mack took the usual walk from the Cintas Center over to the Gallagher Center basement for his weekly radio show. A rookie coach, a 1-2 finish in the Old Spice Classic, and a fan base that only knew winning, wasn't the recipe for a friendly radio show. But Mack was honest, straightforward, and confident. His message to callers was simple; the season isn't a sprint, but a marathon. Xavier's objective was to continue to improve every day they hit the floor. It wasn't a time to question the coaching staff's philosophy, but a time to live it. Continue to preach "Do what we do" to the team. Mack left the show looking forward to Kent State.

Xavier got off the mat a few nights later with a solid home win over Kent State. Led by Jordan Crawford's 21 points, Xavier moved their record to 5-2, again keeping the losing streak at one. Crawford was a scorching 5-of-7 from beyond the 3-point arc. His field goal and 3-point field goal totals were both career highs. Sophomore guard Terrell Holloway was the only other Musketeer in double-figures, scoring 13 points on 3-of-4 shooting. Holloway was also 6-of-7 from the charity stripe, dished-out five assists and recorded three thefts.

Senior center Jason Love had another well-rounded night, scoring 10 points and grabbing 10 rebounds while blocking four shots. The double-double was Love's fourth in the season.

Xavier came from behind to grab a 36-34 halftime lead yet was unable to shake the Golden Flashes in the early goings of the second half. Kent State would manage to pull to within one point, 49-48 at the 14-minute mark; however, Xavier took control of the game with a 13-3 run over the next five minutes and seized a 61-51 lead after Dante Jackson buried a 3-pointer in the corner at the nine-minute mark. Kent State would shrink the Xavier advantage to seven points but Crawford converted on four-straight points to give XU some cushion and effectively put the game away.

Xavier struggled early and Kent State took advantage, jumping out to a 29-17 lead with 6:40 remaining in the first half. Mack spoke to that point, "I was proud of our team tonight. Kent State came out quickly and punched our team in the mouth. It was good to see that we could take their run, and be the team I thought we would be."

One realizes that after watching Mack finish with the media that there really is no rest for a head coach. A trip to Manhattan, Kansas to face Kansas State was already weighing on Mack's mind, "No question this is our toughest test yet. We are going into a tough place to play against a really solid team. We thought ball pressure was tough in the Marquette game, K State will take that to a whole new level. They also have some serious offensive weapons on the floor in Jacob Pullen and Denis Clemente that will require our complete attention on the defensive side of the floor.

"But, I really believe that if we have supreme effort and a good basketball IQ in things like scoring and rebounding we can walk away with a win."

The Kansas State game was Xavier's first big road challenge of the year, they had yet to go on the road and play on an opposing team's floor since everyone at the Old Spice in Florida was on a neutral floor. The environment in Manhattan posed one of the tougher tests in college basketball, and unfortunately, Xavier failed that test. They failed miserably in the two areas that had Mack concerned; scoring and rebounding which led to a loss 71-56.

Both teams struggled to get their offense going in the early part of the contest as Xavier held just a 7-4 margin after a jumper from sophomore Kenny Frease at the 14:08 mark. A three-pointer from Crawford gave Xavier its last lead of the first half, 17-16, with 7:12 remaining in the frame. Outside of a free throw from junior Andrew Taylor, the Musketeers were held scoreless for nearly six minutes until Redford sank two free throws with just over 45 seconds left.

Kansas State headed into the locker room with a 10-point advantage, 30-20. Six Musketeers had tallied two or three fouls in the first half as XU committed 14 fouls to KSU's nine. Mack spoke in the corridor outside the locker room, "I really felt like we were ready to play, but we couldn't get a defensive rebound in the first half. K State shot terrible from the field in the half, but with our guys, most notably Jamel Maclean, in foul trouble, it gave them a lot of second looks which they were able to convert."

In the locker room at the half the message from Mack was simple, "Fellas we played soft under the glass! No poise whatsoever with the ball. But you know what, we are only down ten, we're not out. If we can stop being soft with the ball, and man up on the glass, we can get back in the game. They threw their best at us and they're up 10, not 25. We're fine."

As pumped as the team was coming out for the second half it was not enough to translate to success on the floor as Kansas State stretched its lead to 15, 40-25, three minutes into the second half. Xavier still could not get a shot to drop as it went without a field goal for 6:30 until Kenny Frease completed a three-point play with a layup and free throw to set the score at 46-33 in favor of the Wildcats. Later Brad Redford drained his fourth three of the night to cut the lead to 11, 54-43, with a little more than seven minutes remaining in the contest. Soon thereafter, Xavier pulled within 10, 56-46, at the

6:10 mark after a Crawford layup and subsequent made free throw but they would get no closer.

Later, with just a few minutes remaining on the clock, Mack felt as though the seconds couldn't tick away any faster as he and his staff watched the waning moments of the team's 71—56 loss. The team had been warned that Kansas State was a difficult place to play and that they were going to pressure the ball relentlessly from the opening tip.

That is exactly what happened, and Mack's still growing and inexperienced team was not able to handle their first true road test of the year. "Fellas we just walked out there and got punched in the face," Mack told the team afterward, "If we come out with the same intensity Sunday night against UC the same thing is gonna happen."

Later, sitting on the tarmac, wondering if their charter was going to beat a snowstorm out of Manhattan, Mack spoke. "We just got in too deep, with poor shooting and defensive rebounding hounding us all night; it was too much to overcome.

"I think we got the player's attention though afterwards. When a team loses their antennae goes up a bit more, they tend to focus a bit more on what you are saying. They are gonna need to pay a lot of attention the next couple of days with Cincinnati next on the schedule.

This scenario was exactly what Mack had feared going into arguably the biggest game of his young coaching career; a team on the ropes facing a ranked opponent in the University of Cincinnati at the always hotly contested Crosstown Shootout.

Chapter 4

The Shootout

The series dates back to 1928, when the University of Cincinnati helped St. Xavier College dedicate its brand new, $350,000 Schmidt Fieldhouse, which had a capacity of 4,500. Xavier won the game, 29-25, and the two teams didn't meet again until the 1942-43 season.

The teams began playing on an annual basis starting in 1945-46, and from 1948 to 1958, they played each other twice a year. Since then, UC and XU have played each other once a year, and UC leads the all-time series, 47 games to 29. Xavier, however, had won five of the last seven games.

By the time the team bus made it back to campus in the middle of the night from their charter flight from Manhattan, Mack and his assistants had the team closing the door on their recent loss and beginning to prepare for UC. The team would be off on Wednesday, but the players knew to be ready for a long tough practice on Thursday.

Xavier was 5-3 and staring down the barrel at two huge opponents in the coming week; UC at home on Sunday, and on the road at Butler almost a week later on Saturday. In between, the players were also going to have to deal with the pressure of final exams from the fall semester. Mack knew that the next week was going to be a delicate balancing act of getting the team to stay mentally fresh, get through finals, and somehow be prepared to play these two games.

Even though it was early in the season, Mack knew that if Xavier came out on the losing end of the next two games whispers could start about his performance. By the time the team assembled for practice on Thursday they had all but forgotten the loss from Tuesday night in Manhattan. Many players had endured one-on-one video sessions with assistant coaches Kelsey and Steele to go over their performance and learn what they would need to work on moving forward.

The team had received the advance scouting report for Cincinnati, and Thursday's practice was their first opportunity to begin going over the offensive sets that UC preferred to run and learn how to defend each one. Mack felt like the team needed to get tougher quickly, "If we don't get a little more tough minded we are going to get hammered against UC. They are a big team, the biggest we have faced all year, and we need to be prepared to handle the physicality they are going to bring. Plus it's the Shootout, the one game a year where you walk off the court feeling like you just played a football game."

With that thought in mind the staff decided to begin practice with players taking hard charge fouls under the basket. Mack knew that the drill walked a fine line between being tough and risking injury, but he felt as though it would set the right tone for the coming practice. The team broke out of the charge drill right into some full court offensive drills. Mack was yelling, "We have to be committed to the run, every team says that they play fast, but they don't. Do you have the effort to do it?"

Later Mack switched gears to the defensive side of the ball, rebounding in particular. It was an area where Xavier was manhandled against Kansas State, and success in that part of the game was critical if they were going to beat UC. Cincinnati had the nation's No. 2 rebounding margin, leading their opponents by an average of 12.3 boards, Xavier was plus 6.3.

The drill had three players on the perimeter and one in the lane. One of the coaches would throw the ball to any of the three on the perimeter, who would then shoot. All four players would crash the board. The theory was if one guy could out-rebound three in practice, then he could certainly do it against just one during a game.

"Kansas State killed us on the boards on Tuesday, which cannot happen again on Sunday," Mack said. Minutes later, not liking what he saw early into the drill, Mack stopped things to demonstrate the technique he wanted to see, "Hit him hard with your arm in the chest, turn around and root him out with your butt! You have got to want it more than the other guy!"

Assistant Coach Kelsey chimed in, "We watched the tape of Kansas State and they just punched us in the mouth, are you gonna let that happen again on your home floor?"

Mack again warned about how UC was going to impose their will, "Those boys are going to be ready for you fellas, they want to be physical. You gotta push your man back off the ball! C'mon fellas! What is our mentality? It's defense, and we can't be a good defensive team if we don't rebound! Who is gonna be a warrior? We were soft against Kansas State. 11 offensive rebounds! 11!"

Moments later Mack laid in to Jordan Crawford who appeared to be giving a half-hearted effort, "JC do you know how to rebound?"

Crawford responded, "Yeah coach."

"Then rebound! Where is the effort? I mean what's it going to take for our 2 guard to get a rebound? It's not that hard," Mack replied.

As practice wore on, the players were starting to fatigue, and it showed during a half court offensive drill. Jason Love and Terrell Holloway had had enough of each other; even though they were on the same team for the drill. Their complaining at each other about who should be where on the floor was enough for the whole team to hear, including Mack.

Mack cut in, "What the hell is this, fellas? Stop! We've got enough people questioning what we are doing lately; we don't need to do it to each other. Let's stand together, no more bitching."

The team was exhausted when they walked off the court, but had practiced hard and efficiently for the previous two hours.

"We (the coaching staff) know they can be tough, but they have to believe it themselves if they are to be the stronger team on Sunday night. If they don't stand up to UC it could be a long night," Mack said as the team made its way to the showers.

The Xavier team had a quiet, confident look about themselves as they filed into the locker room for last minute instructions from Mack before facing UC. "Fellas this is a different game. It's a street fight. You will get pushed, you will get shoved. Keep your head up and don't back down," Mack said.

Mack rolled a five minute video showing clips from previous Shootouts in which physical, hard plays usually led to some shoving and pushing. Other clips showed players scrambling for loose balls that ended with a shove or two. Lastly, there were replays when actual punches had been thrown.

The video stopped and the lights came back on to a quiet room.

Mack spoke to the team from the rear of the locker room. "Fellas as you can see, you cannot back down against these guys. You have to be there for each other for forty minutes. It's going to be a physical game, but we need to be tough minded and fearless."

Mack began to raise his voice as he made his way into the middle of the room, looking each player straight in the eye, "What are you willing to do tonight? Afterwards when you are in your dorm room you can't have any regrets! Don't think, 'man if I had done this or that we could have won.' No regrets! Let's get out there and play harder than UC for 40 minutes, nothing less!"

That brought the team up out of their lockers to the middle of the room, "Center X," as it's sometimes called because of the team logo laid in the carpet.

"Fellas let's bring it in here."

The team, now joined as one with their hands raised in the air, looked to their coach one last time, "Fellas, UC has no idea what they are about to get themselves into. Let's go!"

Seconds later the team charged out onto the court for warm-ups. The butterflies were definitely on display on the player's faces during player introductions and the National Anthem. Mack was determined to keep the team focused and upbeat, clapping and encouraging everyone around him, "Let's go fellas, forty minutes, nothing less. No let up the whole night!"

As the players took the floor for the opening tip the arena was barely able to contain the energy. No, this certainly was not like any other game as Mack knew, and decided that it would be the perfect platform to get a message across to Jordan Crawford, "I made a decision in the best interest of the team not to start Jordan. I felt like Jordan could be going harder on both ends of the floor and needed to listen more to the coaches who were trying to coach him."

Seconds later the ball was in the air and Mack's first taste of the Crosstown Shootout as head coach had begun. At the first television timeout Xavier had set the early tone with four blocks and had moved out in front 10 – 4. In the huddle Mack told the players to keep up the level of intensity that they started the game with.

By the next timeout UC, behind solid defense and winning the rebounding battle on both ends of the floor, had forged a tie.

Mack used the timeout to again stress to big men Love and Frease that they needed to be aggressive on both ends of the floor in order for Xavier to stay in the game. The game had gotten a lot more physical as the half wore on. Chip shots on screens and an extra push or shove during a rebound were becoming the norm.

Mack's worry intensified over the next four minutes when Xavier missed four shots on the offensive end and was out-rebounded by UC every time. UC was converting at the offensive end of the floor and making shots at the line when Xavier made some undisciplined fouls.

Mack tensed at the thought of UC starting to pull away, "It was 17-12 in favor of [UC] at that point, I knew we had to answer at one end of the floor or another, and quick."

This was the message that Mack delivered to the team in the huddle, "We need some individuals to step up! Right now! We have to answer." UC was on a 12-0 run and grabbing every rebound in site.

Xavier's answer finally came with a little more than seven minutes left in the half.

As Mack had stressed to the team before the game, "there will come a point when you have to ask yourself, was there anything more I could do to help my team win the game?" Jordan Crawford was the first to answer that question.

After another made UC basket put them up 19-12, Xavier guard Terrell Holloway brought the ball down the floor and was able to work the ball over to Crawford who missed a jumper on the wing. Jason Love was not going to be denied when he went for the rebound. Love grabbed the ball then kicked it underneath to Dante Jackson who missed a layup, grabbed his own rebound and was fouled, hard, going back up to the basket by Cashmere Wright of UC.

That's when Crawford and UC's Rashad Bishop got into it in the lane. Crawford decided he had enough at that point and was not going to back down from the taunts that Bishop was throwing around. Seconds later, all players on the floor were in on the conversation which had the referees scurrying to break things up. Crawford and Bishop were each assessed a technical foul.

Mack said it was the spark the team needed, and like many games against UC in the past, it was born from a situation that went beyond the traditional x's and o's, "I think that situation sent a message to UC that said even though we're down by seven or eight points, this game is not over."

Xavier went on a 12-2 run of their own to pull into the lead 24-21 heading into the last timeout of the half.

The officials called for a television timeout on the UC offensive end of the floor after Xavier's Love committed a foul on UC's Lance Stephenson. As the UC players made their way to their own bench they crossed paths with the Xavier players taking the floor for the timeout. When words were exchanged both teams nearly went at it again. Coaches and players alike raced toward the midcourt line as some jawing, pushing and shoving ensued.

One UC player was inadvertently knocked to the floor by a Bearcats assistant coach, and there was plenty of screaming and pointing by both sides. The officials had enough at that point and brought both together to help calm things down. Mack said, "We were told that if things were not brought under control that, 'we're gonna have to resort to assessing technicals, and you are both going to start losing players for the remainder of the game.'"

"I think at that point both teams had sort of made their own statement and things were pretty calm until halftime," said Mack.

When both teams exited the floor Xavier enjoyed a five-point lead. Mack felt like they had already taken UC's best punch and would be able to withstand whatever came their way in the second half.

In the locker room at the half it was clear that this was the most physical game of the year. The toll it was taking on the team was evident; numerous players were using ice packs and the training staff was working on Terrell Holloway's back which had tightened up before the end of the half.

Mack was upbeat and all business when he came into the room. "Fellas, we won three of five in four minute wars, so let's keep it up in that regard. Stay in the present and we'll be fine." Wars are the term used to describe the score during each four minute interval between television timeouts.

Mack continued, "Here is what we need to do in the second half to win; on defense we've got to do a better job blocking out, if we rebound they can't win! Ball screen defense; we are doing a good job of building walls and cutting them off out near the top of the key and disrupting their offensive flow, keep it up."

Mack switched gears and talked about the offense, "Let's have an unbelievable pace in the 2nd half. They are struggling to keep up with us when we run. When we rebound or start dead ball, clear it out and get down court like your hair is on fire.

"In our half-court offense we need to get the ball down in the post. In 35 possessions in the half we only went into the post seven times, don't stop, and get it in there. This guy, Love, has eleven rebounds already; reward him in the 2nd half."

The team responded to Mack's halftime assessment and at the fourteen minute mark of the second half had opened the lead to ten. Neither team was executing very well on the offensive side of the ball, and with all of the missed shots, rebounding was becoming even more critical. Xavier was trying to do what Mack said at the half, to get the ball inside, and was starting to have success.

Half of Xavier's points in the early part of the second half were coming from inside the lane. Mack knew that if Xavier could pose a threat to score from both inside and out they were going to be tough to stop. UC wouldn't quit though, and battled back to forge a tie as the game clock crept under eight minutes remaining. The score went back and forth over the next four minutes with Xavier clinging to a two point lead when Kenny Frease fouled Yancy Gates with one minute showing on the clock. Gates, despite the ear-splitting noise from the Xavier home crowd, calmly sank both free throws to knot the score at 59-59.

Xavier ran a half court play that got the ball to Terrell Holloway for the go ahead shot, which he made. Despite the bedlam in the arena, UC quickly got the ball back down the court to Lance Stephenson who made a jumper from the outside to once again tie the score with just 14 seconds left.

Mack decided to let things play out as he encouraged his team to hustle back down to their end of the floor. After a series of screens near the three point line Holloway once again found the ball in his hands and a chance to win the game.

Holloway got off a clear shot, but was off the mark. Dante Jackson had been streaking through the lane when he grabbed the rebound, then turned and put up a fade away shot from in the lane.

The shot by Jackson went in, and the entire arena erupted. But no sooner had the ball made it through the net, the officials were racing to the scoring table to wave the shot off. They claimed that Jackson had not released the ball before the game clock expired, which was clearly the right call.

The Shootout was headed to overtime.

Mack remained composed, not getting caught up in the moment as he assessed his players' foul situation and number of timeouts. Mack then regrouped the team for instructions. UC was still winning the war in the paint, so Mack once again stressed the importance of getting the ball inside. UC was also tiring as the game went on and Mack reiterated pace and to push the ball for the next five minutes.

UC jumped out to a quick four point lead behind field goals from both Lance Stephenson and Yancy Gates. Xavier's Mark Lyons responded with two shots of his own and the score was tied with three minutes to go.

Two missed jumpers by Jordan Crawford allowed UC to get the ball in transition and push the lead to five with just under one minute to go. Xavier pushed the ball up the court and Holloway was fouled driving to the basket. After making both free throws, Mack called timeout. "I didn't really like our chances with a minute to go, but Terell's made free throws were clutch and sort of got that killer look back in our player's eyes."

Mack stressed urgency on the defensive end of the floor and it paid off during UC's next possession. Jason Love stripped the ball from Rashad Bishop and hit Terrell Holloway in transition before being fouled. Holloway, who was leading the A-10 in free throw percentage, made both to pull Xavier within one.

On UC's next possession Dante Jackson fouled Dixon who made two of his own giving UC a three point lead with just 25 seconds left. Terrell Holloway had perhaps the play of the game when he drove the ball down the court, cut across the lane and headed straight to the rim. Holloway shot, was fouled, then shouted to the rafters as the ball fell through the basket. Holloway then made the free throw to complete the three-point play and tie the game.

UC got the ball to their end of the floor and called timeout with eight seconds left to set up the game winning play. It was no surprise that the ball ended up in the hands of Lance Stephenson who shot the ball with three seconds left, and missed. After the ball tipped around between a couple of players Xavier's Jordan Crawford cradled it in his arms as the clock struck zero. For the first time in the history of the Shootout the game was going into double overtime.

"I felt that overcoming the deficit that we did with so little time left sort of told the team that there was nothing we couldn't overcome. It was like UC kept throwing haymakers, and we just simply wouldn't go down. Our kids weren't going to fold. If it took 50 minutes, it took 50 minutes. Play to win," said Mack.

When UC's Yancy Gates made a shot with a little over three minutes to go it put UC up by three. UC had again taken charge, as they had in the first overtime, and put Xavier well behind the eight ball with time running out. This time though, the outcome would be different, Yates had just made UC's last basket of the night.

Jordan Crawford made one of two free throws after being fouled in the act of shooting, then, on the next possession fed Jason Love down low for the basket. In less than one minute Xavier had tied the game.

The action reached a furious level on UC's next trip down the floor in which they missed three shots and got all three rebounds before Xavier's Andrew Taylor fouled UC's Steve Toyloy, who had only seen ten minutes of action the whole night. Toyloy had not been to the free throw line to that point, and it showed, when he missed both free throws.

Xavier got the rebound and quickly pushed the ball up the floor. Holloway fed Love down low for the score and Xavier held the lead by two. It was the first time in either overtime period that Xavier had the lead.

UC missed on their ensuing possession then fouled Jason Love with less than ten seconds to play. Love confidently walked to the other end of the floor, sank both free throws and put the game out of reach.

When the clock expired Mack's assistants were patting him on the back and giving him high fives. Mack made his way towards the UC coaching staff and team to shake hands, all the while looking as though he had just survived a plane crash. Xavier players celebrated with a victory lap around the court before slapping hands with the student section as they made their way to the locker room.

Love, who had just played in his last Shootout, praised his team-mates who made the win possible, "It was one of the most intense games I've played in," Love said. "I'm so proud of these guys. They helped me go out the right way against UC, being 3-1. I just can't say enough. We showed toughness and togetherness. We were down and we looked bad and we stayed with it." Love tied career highs with 19 rebounds and five blocks, and scored seven points.

Sophomore guard Terrell Holloway paced XU with a career-high 26 points and was 11-of-11 from the free-throw line. Free throws were ultimately the difference, as XU made 28 of 36 attempts and UC connected on 10 of 22. "We wanted to get to the free throw line," UC guard Deonta Vaughn said. "We wanted to get to the free throw line a lot, but you have to make it. When we got there, we couldn't make it."

Xavier had responded to Mack's pre-game plea to do whatever it took to win the game, and most importantly, not back down from UC's physical style of play. Jordan Crawford, who added 16 points and six rebounds, insisted that the game was never near blows. "They tried to come in and be the bullies, and we wanted to be the bullies too. We ain't going to back down from nobody," he said. "All of that was – we're not backing down from them. We put them on their heels a little bit."

"My guys lost their cool, no doubt about it," UC coach Mick

Cronin said. "We went from up seven (points) to down five because of that ruckus ..."

When the whole team made it to the locker room there was still a lot of cheering and laughter to go around. Mack felt it was the right thing to do to give the team a few extra moments to savor the win. When Mack came into a locker room, which was packed with additional Xavier administration and recruits, he sarcastically quipped, "I knew we had that one in the bag the whole time," as laughter filled the locker room

Mack walked to the head of the room and dropped to one knee as he led the team in their customary post-game prayer. When the prayer was complete, Mack stayed put for an extra second or two to let the moment sink in before addressing the team, "Guys, great job. I've been around a lot of these (shootouts) as a fan, player, and coach, and that was the best Crosstown Shootout I've ever seen. When you talk to the media, talk about our team and how proud you are of what we did, don't talk negative about [UC], we have to play this game every year.

"We learned a lot tonight about toughness, we were not tough at Kansas State, but we were tonight, and if we keep doing that, we can have a lot of special nights like this the rest of the year. Remember our team motto is 'Do what we do', tonight we did, and because of that we get to send UC 2-1/2 miles back to the other side of town with a loss!"

In the coaches locker room Mack was finally able to catch his breath after media sessions with local radio and print media. Always the coach, Mack was quick to point out the things that the team needed to work on, "We're not quite there yet with things like our intensity off the ball, our awareness off the ball, and our perimeter players executing block outs, so we'll make sure to focus on those things this week because we will need to get better in those areas if we want to beat Butler next Saturday."

Mack was also frustrated by the lackluster play of Jamel McLean who played nineteen minutes and came away with only one point and five rebounds. "He hasn't played to his ability level the last couple of games," Mack said. "We are really counting on him to have a great junior year. We need production, defense, and solid (play) around the basket...and he is so capable of doing those three things."

Mack stared into his locker and said, "Tonight was a big win, a great win, and one that I'll enjoy, but let's face it, we're 6-3 and looking at playing a ranked opponent on the road in six days. There's still a lot of work to be done." Mack left for his office upstairs to pick up video from the game before heading home, already consumed with how to get the next win.

Chris as a toddler, just learning to walk, but already has a basketball in his hands.

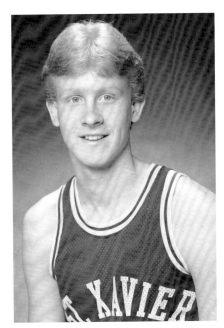

Chris Mack as a senior at St. Xavier High School.

Chris recovering from his second knee surgery. He blew out both knees while at Xavier.

Chris Mack and his family are all smiles before the press conference to announce his hiring as the new head basketball coach at Xavier.

Coach Mack speaks to the press while Athletic Director Mike Bobinski looks on.

Photos by Greg Rust, Xavier University

Coach Chris Mack and his staff discuss strategy during a timeout.

Lyons drives hard from the wing against Rhode Island.

Jordan Crawford scores two more vs. Rhode Island.

Coach Mack calling in plays.

Jordan Crawford looks for an opening against Cincinnati.

Jason Love blocking a shot against Cincinnati.

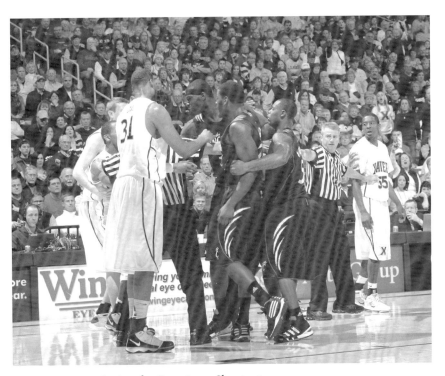

A tense moment during the Crosstown Shootout

Dante Jackson revs up the crowd.

Brad Redford prepares to
make another three-pointer.

Dante Jackson disrupts another play on defense vs. Dayton.

Jason Love driving hard to the basket.

Dante Jackson penetrates the Dayton defense.

McLean floats toward the rim for a hard fought two points vs. LSU.

Kenny Frease shoots from the lane against Duquesne.

Jason Love takes on two LSU defenders trying for the rebound.

Terrell Holloway brings the ball up the floor.

Mark Lyons works free for an open layup.

Jamel McLean taking flight.

Jamel McLean goes above the rim for a rebound against St. Joseph's.

Chapter 5

The Clock

With the Crosstown Shootout in the rearview mirror Mack focused his attention to the next opponent on the schedule, the Indianapolis based Butler Bulldogs. Butler had continued to barge onto the national scene by playing well in the NCAA Tournament the last few years, very similar to how Gonzaga obtained national recognition in the late 90's. Butler, much like Xavier, was always looking to schedule solid home and away games; this would be one of those games for both teams. The winner of the upcoming game would be able to chalk up a strong win on the NCAA resume come March.

Adding to the aura of the game was the arena itself, Hinkle Fieldhouse. Probably best known for the scenes filmed during the making of *Hoosiers* in the mid 1980's which chronicled the story of tiny Milan High School winning the Indiana State Championship. Hinkle had an old crusty, tiny gym feel that made you feel as if you were watching a game back in the day. It almost felt as if someone was going to break out the peach baskets before tipoff.

Mack and his team were having none of the syrupy feelings most Xavier fans were as they made their way up I-74 from Cincinnati to watch the game. Mack was here to win a basketball game, plain and simple. The week after the UC game had been finals week at Xavier. That meant Monday was a reading day and Tuesday was exams, so no practice either day. "That probably wasn't such a bad thing, our players needed the rest, the UC game was pretty physical," said Mack.

The players and coaches filed on to the bus one at a time, set to make the 90-minute drive to Indianapolis the day before the Butler game. The bus would go directly to Hinkle Fieldhouse for the players to take in a light shoot around. Mack, like most coaches, is intent on having his players get a feel for the court and its surroundings before taking the court for real the next day. Being that Saturday's start was 2pm, Xavier opted to not use their 9am shooting time on Saturday.

It was a relaxed evening at Hinkle. Mack broke the team up into two groups with post players at one end of the floor and guards at the other. A few friendly shooting competitions between the two groups were orchestrated by coaches Steele and Kelsey, with Mack laying the ground rules. The guards began to tease their post playing counterparts as they won the first few contests. It was all in fun. Mack had kept the team focused and loose, the balance every coach in America tries to pull off.

The players made their way to center court when Mack cried out, "Bring it in!" The team was quiet as Mack instructed them on being ready, knowing their assignments, and getting the proper rest later that evening. The players drew closer as everyone raised their hands along with Mack and yelled, "1,2,3, Attack!"

Quickly, players beckoned student managers to throw them basketballs as the team formed a single file line behind Dante Jackson; an informal shooting contest was about to begin. Coaches sat on the scorer's table and watched player after player heave half court shots with mixed results. Five shooters in, Jordan Crawford took two dribbles and in one motion let go a high arching one handed push shot all the while watching the ball's flight. As the ball trickled through the net Crawford exclaimed, "It's over!" And with that, the players headed for the bus.

The next afternoon the players gathered in the dingy basement locker room for last minute instructions. The sound from the Butler band could be heard echoing down the hallway just outside, but it was not a distraction to the players, all eyes were intently focused on Mack, "Fellas, we're here, we're in the lion's den. They are waiting for us upstairs but have no idea what they are about to get into. I want you to go out, forget the band, the fans, the Fieldhouse, and

Bobby Knight on ESPN, let's just focus on being fearless and being the aggressor. Let's be smart with the ball, get good shots. I don't want any three's in the first four minutes unless you are wide open."

Butler was equipped with All American talent throughout their starting lineup, so Mack felt it was important to go over some personnel thoughts one more time, "Jordan, you are guarding Nored, watch him driving into the paint, he will pass more often than shoot. Terrell, Shelvin Mack could be 1 for 9 or 9 for 11. Remember to force his dribble to his weak side, which is right. Cheeks(Lyons), Gordon Hayward is tough to defend, but use your quickness and get underneath him and you'll be fine. Dante, Veasley will want to crash the boards, block him out and use ball screens against him on offense. Jason Love, be strong against Howard, there's no way that he can block your shot. Remember we're in their house, are we going to tiptoe in or bring a spear? C'mon, let's go get it done."

With that message the team charged up the stairs and out into the bright lights and blaring sounds of a packed Hinkle Fieldhouse. It was a scene that seemed to capture everything that is great about college basketball.

Four minutes into the game Mack could have cared less. Xavier obviously forgot the spear and was looking up at a 16-4 deficit before the first TV timeout. Mack's words of encouragement didn't seem to help much. When the first official timeout came, Xavier was still down 12 points, 20-8.

Butler opened the game shooting a blistering 75 percent from the field to XU's 33.3 percent in the first five minutes of action. Butler's hot streak continued with a 20-6 run in the first eight minutes of the game. The Musketeers trailed by as much as 15, but a 12-5 Xavier run in the last five minutes of the half cut the Butler lead to just seven points. Brad Redford led the Musketeer scoring in the first frame with eight points including two big threes.

Xavier trailed 39-32 at halftime.

Mack was pleased that his team composed themselves on the floor, but did not like what he saw when he reached the locker room. Lyons, Holloway, and Crawford were jawing back and forth about missed assignments in the first half. As Mack made his way through the cramped room to an office back near the showers where he would confer with his staff, he yelled to the team, "The complaining to each other stops, and I mean now."

Silence filled the room while Mack and the rest of the staff huddled together near the showers. When finished, Mack strode to the front of the room to instruct the team on second half strategy, "All right fellas, listen up. We did a great job to get back in the game, we're only down seven, and just starting to play. They came out ready, but we've clawed back, so do what we do in the second half and we'll be fine. Now, on defense, we have to show more ball pressure. We need to crowd certain parts of the floor, make it hard for them to move around without the ball.

"On offense, you need to understand something, if you are standing around, you are killing the team. We have to have better movement away from the ball. When you hold the ball Butler packs down and crowds the lane. We can't have that, Kenny and Jason had 26 points and 11 boards between them. They got those points at the midway point in the half when we were moving the ball. Early in the game with no movement, we never got the ball in. That is a big key for the second half. "

Mario Mercurio yelled from the back of the room, "Coach under four minutes!" That meant Mack had to wrap it up pretty quick. "OK, fellas, last thing, let's keep the pace up the entire time, we were slow to start, stay quick from the get go. Let's go." This time the players listened. Xavier came out of the gate in the second half with a 9-0 run to take the lead at the 17:37 mark with a trey from sophomore Jordan Crawford to put the score at 41-39 in favor of the Musketeers.

Butler battled back into the game at the 12:01 mark on a Willie Veasley layup to cut the Xavier lead to one. A Kenny Frease layup with 11:25 remaining gave Xavier a 54-51 lead, but Butler pulled within three, 56-53, on a Shelvin Mack lay-in at the 8:14 mark.

Two free throws by Ronald Nored with 4:07 left in the game tied the score at 60. The two teams traded blows until the end with Crawford hitting a two with 46-seconds left to give the Musketeers a 68-65 lead. That's when things really got interesting.

On Butler's ensuing possession Shelvin Mack was fouled on a questionable hand check, went to the line and made both free throws, cutting the lead to one, 68-67. Xavier struggled to get the ball inbounds, and finally did to Mark Lyons. Lyons bobbled the ball and bit, and depending on whose side you were on, was either fouled or tied up in a loose ball that would determine possession. The referee crew saw it Butler's way and called a jump ball. The possession arrow showed Butler, the Bulldogs would have the ball, down one with 38.5 seconds left.

The next thirty seconds were a mad skirmish that saw Butler get off a shot that was almost rebounded by Kenny Frease. Frease couldn't get a handle on the ball, though, which was knocked into the backcourt where Butler regained possession. As the time wound down under ten seconds, the clock seemed to stop briefly, but play continued. Butler got off another shot that was missed, but Gordon Hayward got the rebound and put the ball in for the go ahead basket with 1.2 seconds showing on the clock.

As Hinkle Fieldhouse erupted Mack called a timeout, and then was told by assistant Brian Thornton that the clock had stopped briefly. Mack wanted to discuss the clock stoppage with the officiating crew.

"I asked Brian is he was sure, he said he was. I had asked him how long and he thought a couple of seconds. I thought if that was the case Hayward's shot should not count. I got one of the officials over and said, 'Listen you need to review that play, the clock stopped when the ball went in the backcourt,'" said Mack. The officials said they would review the play, but since Hinkle Fieldhouse was not equipped with Precision Time, it was going to take some time to sort things out.

Xavier, like all Atlantic 10 men's basketball programs, uses the Precision Time System, which features belt packs worn by officials to signal game clock starts and stops. It includes microphones that halt the clock when whistles are blown. Leagues that adopt Precision Time require all their programs to use it, but it is not mandated by the NCAA. The Horizon League had not adopted this program, therefore Butler was not required to have Precision Timing at Hinkle Fieldhouse.

Mack said, "I thought the officials had a sort of sick look on their faces as they started to figure things out. Initially it looked like they might wave off the basket and the game would be over in our favor."

As more and more time went by the crowd started to get restless. "I figured we better be prepared for the worst, that they wouldn't call the basket off and we needed to have a play ready for the final 1.2 seconds. We went through a couple of scenarios with the players, something that we could run if time allowed, or a tip play in case there were a couple of tenths left on," said Mack of the wait.

The officials finally stepped away from the scorer's table to confer amongst themselves then finally pulled both coaches together to inform them of their final decision. The officials ruled that 1.3 seconds elapsed during the erroneous stoppage, and since Hayward's shot was released at 1.8 seconds, the ball went through the net at 1.2 seconds. Since the game clock had stopped for those 1.3 seconds, that time is deducted from the remaining 1.2 seconds, thus ending the game with Butler the winner.

Chaos ensued throughout the arena, Butler fans cheered at the good news; Xavier fans were incredulous at the bad. Mack had to be restrained from the referees who were making a quick exit from the floor. As the angry players made their way from the floor to the locker room a few players were restrained by team officials as jawing between the fans and the players escalated. The players carried their tirade downstairs into the locker room tearing a water fountain from the wall.

Mack and his staff finally made their way down the long stairwell and stood silent on the bottom landing before addressing the team. At that moment, the pressure of the situation, and possibly a season that was starting to slip away, got to Mack who was screaming and kicking a door, lamenting the fact that he should have called timeout after Butler made the two free throws to cut the lead to one.

"I felt in retrospect that I should have called timeout and set up an inbounds play to get the ball into Terrell's hands, but I didn't and Butler ended up getting the possession call," said Mack.

As the entire coaching staff stood there, along with both Sister Fleming and Mike Bobinski, heads were hung low and not a word was spoken. The only sound breaking the silence was the water spewing forth from the wall in the hallway where a drinking fountain had been.

The water was working its way across the floor towards the staff.

It seemed to serve as a symbol of a tide that had turned against them which had just dropped the team to 6-4.

Mack had to collect himself a bit before addressing the team, when he did it was a somber moment with many tears in the room, "Fellas, that was as tough a loss as I've ever been part of. But let's face it, while we did a lot of things right today, we still needed to do more at the end. When we have a chance to close things out we have to do it. We have to learn from this, be better at end game situations, and we'll make a point of that in practice. When you talk to the media speak well of Butler, then let's get our stuff together and get on the bus."

Mack trudged back up the long flight of stairs to meet with the media, something that was never fun to do after a loss, to discuss at length how the game ended. Mack believed the clock stopped three times in the final minute, and twice in the last possession. As officials evaluated the situation, Mack said Xavier hoped Hayward didn't have enough time to release the ball. "Our director of basketball operations, Brian Thornton, and our associate head coach, Pat Kelsey, were adamant, 'Hey Chris. The clock stopped twice during that last possession.' I don't know the inner-workings of the rule but I do know that if the game goes over 40 minutes, you can't count a shot that would go beyond that," Mack said. Mack stopped short of saying he disagreed with the ruling, but said he was obviously frustrated.

"I know when we go back and I have a chance to watch it on film, I really hope for everybody's sake that they got it right," Mack said. Mack reiterated that his team had plenty of chances to change the game's outcome, from avoiding a tie-up on their last in-bounds play to reeling in loose balls in the final seconds. "The team must learn from the experience," he said, "and blaming others will only stop progress. You can't cry over spilled milk. It's over. We have to put it behind us."

Xavier athletic director Mike Bobinski later said officials correctly followed procedure by reviewing the possession at the ensuing dead ball. Referees D.J. Carstensen, Sid Rodeheffer and Bo Borowski watched replays with a stopwatch.

"The overriding emotion for all involved - this goes for us and I talked to Brad Stevens, Butler's coach, afterward - is that it's just a shame that's the way the game came to that conclusion," Bobinski said. "That was such an unsatisfying way to end a game."

Post-game speculation about additional clock stoppage in the last minute was moot because officials cannot go back multiple possessions to evaluate stops once play has resumed.

Bobinski talked to John Adams, the NCAA coordinator of men's basketball officiating, and Horizon League commissioner Jonathan LeCrone, among others. "There was 'no true mechanism' for Xavier to pursue anything further," Bobinski said, "We talked to everyone we needed to talk to about it."

It was a long, quiet bus ride back to Cincinnati. Coaches normally made a habit of watching that day's game on the laptop on the return trip. This bus ride would be different. Coaches and players alike stared out the window as the bus made its way along I-74. About 50 minutes into the trip, Mack motioned to Justin Faris, the team's video coordinator, to bring his computer to the front of the bus.

As Mack examined the last few possessions, he would shake his head in disbelief and continue replaying Butler's final possession. While fans would go on to debate the time keeper's error, Mack was frustrated by Xavier's missed opportunities to end the game. Butler managed to get off two shots on the game's final possession. Loose balls on the floor were controlled by Butler on two occasions.

Mack slowly made his way to the end of the bus in search of Mark Lyons. Lyons looked up and straightened in his seat when he saw Mack approach. Mack talked to his young freshman about the importance of not leaving any gray area for an official. During end of the game situations Mack told Lyons that he needed to catch the ball with his elbows out, and not let the defender reach in and create a tie up, like Gordon Hayward had done to Lyons earlier.

It was a classic teaching moment from coach to player. "Be strong, draw the foul. Never curl up and hunch over the ball. You're just inviting a tough call for the official to make," Mack instructed. Lyons nodded with understanding as Mack continued, "I don't think it was the right call Cheeks, but next time you're in that position, make it easy for the official and we'll get that call."

Mack retraced his steps to the front of the bus to sit through 30 more minutes of silence as the bus continued to hum along towards Cincinnati.

The team met briefly at the Cintas Center before going their separate ways. Mack told the team that they had no choice but to move on, they had Miami coming into town and would begin preparing for them the next day with free throws and some overview of their personnel. After everyone had filed out Mack made his way up to his office that has a balcony that overlooks the court. Staring down at the court where just six days earlier Mack and his team felt the jubilation of their double overtime victory over rival Cincinnati, Mack couldn't help but feel the depth of the other side of the coin in his profession, the losing.

Losing the way the team did earlier in the day made things that much harder, but as he instructed his players a short time ago, Mack himself had to let it go and move on; there were always more games to be played.

Chapter 6

Happy Holidays?

In the locker room before the Miami game tension filled the air. The players knew that a win would finally put the Butler game in the rearview mirror. The team was also faced with a self-imposed pressure of sorts; win this last game going into Christmas break.

The last three years Xavier had lost the game before break setting a sour mood for the holiday. Mack's staff had commented how important it was to get a win at this point in the season, to really be able to relax and enjoy the time off, instead of fretting over a recent loss and questioning where the team's focus is. It was no joke; the team was not taking this game lightly at all.

Mack came into the room about ten minutes prior to tipoff, "Fellas let's talk defense. Remember tonight is like every other game, a series of ten-four minute wars. Just focus on what we need to do the next four minutes until the next official timeout. If we do that things will take care of themselves."

Mack was a huge believer in this philosophy of trying to shrink the game down into smaller periods of time, "It intensifies your focus as both a coach and a player. Don't look at the game as a whole, just look at what is going to happen from now until the next timeout. Pretty soon we'll be out of time and walk out with a win."

Mack continued talking about defense, "Fellas, we need to achieve seven kills on defense. In our last three games we had kills of 2, 3, and 2, and were 1-2. In our five games where we got seven kills we were 4-1. On average, over the course of a season when we get seven kills a game we will win 96% of the time, believe me on that."

Kills are defined as stopping an opponent from scoring on three straight possessions. When that happens it really allows a team to widen the margin as the game unfolds. Mack and his staff gathered much of their belief through Tony Bennett while he was the head coach at Washington State. For years Bennett's father, Dick, was the most respected defensive minded coach in the game. Seven kills was on the dry erase board every time Xavier played, the night of the Miami game would be no different.

"Let's play hard and play together. Miami will take a lot of three's, but they don't make a lot, and are not a real deep team. Let's make them a one shot team tonight. Lastly, let's play hard tonight. I want guys running hard in and out of the game; I want guys yanking guys off the ground after charges. Butler had us down early and in an uneasy position when we played up there, let's return the favor to our opponent tonight!"

Both teams started a bit sluggish even though Xavier had jumped out to a 5-0 lead. Mack seemed pretty quiet during the early part of the game taking notice of numerous things on the court. Jordan Crawford was playing with a lot of energy on the defensive side of the ball, "Way to front your man JC, keep it up."

Mack would occasionally get on the officials a time or two, but nothing over the top, "Guys you need to be making these calls both ways. Both teams are similar right now, we are running a bunch of ball screens like they are; you can't call moving fouls on us and not them."

As the half wore on Xavier started taking some bad shots and getting lazy with the ball, "C'mon fellas, pass and move, move around without the ball to create good shots. Let's watch out how we handle the ball, pay attention, and on defense when you go for a rebound hold onto the damn ball. Grab it with some authority," Mack told the team during the last timeout.

Xavier's poor play let Miami back into the game, cutting the lead to fewer than ten at the half. Mack was not pleased at the half, "Are you kidding me?! Up 18 and we let them back in the game? Put these guys away, we should be up 30 points right now," Mack thundered.

"Guys it's the little things. Jamel, when you get a rebound stop holding the ball, get it to the outlet man and get down the floor. Mark Lyons, you simply need to show up. Jason Love, you have to get nasty when you decide to go for a rebound. You have to say, 'that's my rebound', and get the damn ball. Now, some quick thoughts for the second half; on offense get the damn rebound off a miss. Their man Hayes has ten, that's too many. Have some pace, move the ball. We talked about that during our timeouts. Get the ball down the floor in transition, and more movement in the half court. Watch your passes, don't get lazy, Miami is quick at jumping your passing lanes, be careful. Miami is a pack line team; they play defense under the three point line, drive the ball on them.

"On defense we need to be up on them tighter, simple as that. They are not a good shooting team, so get in their face and apply ball pressure," Mack concluded.

The players were determined not to let this one slip away. They did everything asked of them in the second half, but they still couldn't open a sizable lead. Mack kept imploring his team to push the tempo, "Guys, these guys are winded right now, run them into the floor."

Xavier seemed to shake the Red Hawks with a 15-6 run in the latter stages of the second half and took a 64-56 lead with 3:10 to go. However, in the theme of the night, the trailing team battled back. Miami's Rodney Haddix buried a 3-pointer on the ensuing possession and Orlando Williams knocked down another long-ball at the 1:30 mark to pull Miami within two points, 64-62.

Jason Love made a couple of big free throws on Xavier's next possession, but Kenny Hayes made Miami's tenth 3-pointer of the game with 38-seconds remaining to pull the Red Hawks within just one point, 66-65. Jordan Crawford was fouled on the next two possessions, and knocked down all four foul shots to seemingly put the game away. Miami, however, quickly moved down the floor and scored on a Kenny Hayes layup to cut the lead to three. Miami pressed off the made basket and forced Xavier to turn the ball over.

Miami quickly inbounded the ball, which was stolen by Dante Jackson to ice the game away. Jackson was running down the court with his arms raised, celebrating the win. That's when the unthinkable happened.

One of the officials, D.J Carstensen (and yes as luck would have it, Carstensen was part of the officiating crew at the Butler game) came running across mid court waving off the play saying that the clock shouldn't have started because Xavier was substituting a player into the game.

"Are you kidding me? A clock malfunctions for the second game in a row? I thought I was on Candid Camera," said Mack afterward to Athletic Director Mike Bobinski in the hallway outside of Xavier's locker room.

When order was restored the entire arena held its collective breath as Miami inbounded the ball to Kenny Hayes who was able to get off a three pointer for the tie with two seconds left, but missed. In the locker room after the game Mack cut short the celebration, "Guys, enjoy this win tonight, but understand we have a lot to work on, especially in game ending situations. We have to play better, and smarter down the stretch; the last minute and a half at Butler, and again tonight. We have to improve in this area; games are not won by 30 points in March.

"I want you to go home and enjoy your time with family and friends, be smart about what you do, and be back here by 6:30 on the 26th. We'll start getting ready for LSU then. We have lost at home to Bucknell, Tennessee and Butler here the last three years in the last game before Christmas, so let's be thankful for a pre-Christmas win. Be safe everyone."

No one will ever know, but you had to wonder if Xavier had somehow lost that game, not just because they gave away a huge lead, but lost in the waning seconds due to another heartbreaking clock disruption, what would have happened to the whole season. Instead, it worked out, and Xavier got an early Christmas present, a win, that moved their record to 7-4.

The next few days Mack and his family headed to Louisville to spend time with his wife's family before Christmas. During the break the annual trip to the bowling alley once again commenced between Mack and his wife Christi. As usual Christi would thrash Mack on the lanes revealing her younger days when she accompanied her mom to work at a bowling alley, "I haven't beaten her in three years and it's really starting to get to me. She doesn't even roll it hard," said Mack after his losing effort.

Mack was back in Cincinnati for Christmas day, opening presents at his northern Kentucky home in the morning with his side of the family. Mack's festive mood could not be replaced, and winning the game before Christmas was a welcome change. Pockets of time though, stealing away whenever he could, found Mack on his laptop watching footage of LSU in preparation for the game later that week.

The season was already about a third of the way over and Mack talked about some of the challenges he faced so far as head coach, "Just learning the personality of this team. And I think that challenge would be there no matter who was the head coach. Again, we have so many different parts – I think we have obviously a couple players that didn't even play for us last year. We have several players that are in different roles than they were last year. Maybe they played eight to 10 minutes and now they're playing 17 to 20. Maybe we're asking them to score a little bit more, like a Jason Love, than we've asked him in the past. So I think the challenge for me whether I've been an assistant coach or a head coach now is just learning the personality of this team and trying to figure out the best way to improve it and move it forward as the season goes on."

Oftentimes Mack was asked to grade his personal performance to date which he never allowed himself to do, it is always about the next team, the next game, "I'm hard on myself so I'm not going to give myself a letter grade. But trust me when I tell you, every day (I) watch tape, whether it's our team or an opponent and try to continue to figure out the best way to coach this team. I'll worry about evaluating myself later."

Mack stood before the team minutes prior to the LSU game, "At some point when you were recruited people had to wonder if you were nasty or not. Did you have that mean streak in you when you were down to claw back and win the game, doing whatever it takes? Tonight I want you to be nasty. Again, ten four minute wars, no let up the whole night. I'm sick of letting teams back into the game because of our mistakes. Let's handle our business tonight."

Mack finished with this thought, "How many in here have heard of James Worthy, played on the Lakers with Magic and at North Carolina with Jordan?" Most of the players nodded, acknowledging they knew who Worthy was.

"Does anyone remember his nickname?"

No reply.

"I do, it was Big Game James. You know why? Because anytime you saw Laker highlights it was Magic running the break, or Kareem shooting a skyhook, but when it came to crucial games, ones which determined a playoff series, Worthy was the guy to get it done. He was that guy because he was nasty. Again, I want to you to be nasty, bring your own version of Big Game James to the floor tonight."

Even though Xavier went out and won the first war 9-6, Mack was frustrated with the play of his junior forward, Jamel McLean. McLean had been in a funk lately with little to no production at both ends of the floor. Mack needed McLean to insert himself into the offense a bit more to get some of the emphasis off of Love and Crawford. Lately Mack had fallen into micromanaging McLean's almost every move.

Shortly after checking into the game McLean turned the ball over in the lane and immediately looked over at Mack who had his hands on his head, looking at McLean as if to say, 'are you kidding me, this is what we have been talking about.'

McLean later made a dumb foul that resulted in a three point play. Mack was smacking his hands together telling McLean to use his head more. McLean came around as the half wore on, getting a fist pump from Mack after slamming down a huge dunk that kept Xavier in control of the game.

At the half Xavier had pushed out to a "nasty" 16 point lead. Mack told the team to stay on it; they were doing a good job, but needed to keep that killer instinct in the second half.

The only point Mack made in the locker room was to reemphasize pace, "LSU has not played a team like you yet this year, they are tired, keep running them into the ground. On defense LSU likes to curl around on a lot of their screens, pay attention and stay attached to your man. Let's help each other and crowd the floor a bit more in the next half."

Xavier poured it on right out of the gate and had pushed the lead to 20 points before the first official timeout at the 16 minute mark. From there everything seemed to fall into place as Xavier cruised to an 89-65 win handing LSU their worst loss of the season. Everyone seemingly got in on the act; sophomore guard Terrell Holloway poured in 20 points to lead four Musketeers in double figures. Holloway's 20 came on 5-of-10 shooting and he was an automatic 9-of-9 from the free throw line. He also dished-out six assists, which was one shy of his career high.

Sophomore guard Jordan Crawford scored 17 points on 5-of-13 shooting and was 5-of-5 effort from the free throw line. Jason Love chipped in with 11 points and seven rebounds, and freshman guard Mark Lyons added 12 points and chased down four rebounds. Jamel McLean finally came to and delivered a solid overall effort posting a double-double with 10 points and 10 rebounds. McLean was 4-of-6 from the floor on the night. Sophomore guard Kenny Frease scored seven points and hauled in a career-high 12 rebounds, nine of which came in the first half.

"Great job tonight guys," Mack said to the team afterward, "you killed them on the boards and that is all about effort. We were the bigger, stronger, nastier team tonight for sure. Tonight we didn't shoot as well, but we did some other things to overcome that. Jamel that was a huge game; Terrell, probably your best game in a Xavier uniform."

Mack wrapped things up with some words about the next opponent Wake Forest. There was going to be a lot of hoopla surrounding the game since it was the initial "Skip Prosser Classic." An arrangement had been made between the two schools to do a home and home series for the next ten years to honor the legacy of the former coach.

"Sunday we are at Wake Forest. No question it will be emotional, but come game time it's over and we are there to bust their ass. We have a good chance to steal one from them, their students will still be out on break, and many others are just waiting for ACC season to start.

"Believe me, there are a lot of North Carolina fans that have season tickets to Wake Forest just so they can attend the game when the Tar Heels come to town. Wake gets accused of having a crowd that sits on their hands from time to time, so the atmosphere could be in our favor.

"They are not a good shooting team, so if we defend like we know we can, we can frustrate them. Beat Wake and we'll be 9-4 with a good RPI heading into conference play."

It was the first time Mack had mentioned anything about the RPI, ratings percentage index, which had become a popular metric used by the NCAA Tournament Selection Committee to determine who received at-large bids. Heading into the Wake Forest game Xavier was ranked 36th, and had the 12th best strength-of-schedule.

To that point in the season, many individuals on the team had some noteworthy accomplishments; Xavier sophomore Terrell Holloway led the Atlantic 10 Conference in assist-to-turnover ratio at 3.46-to-1.00, and in free-throw percentage at 88.1 percent (37-of-42).

Kenny Frease made his first collegiate start against LSU and collected a career-high 12 rebounds. It marked his second straight game for Frease to post a career high, having grabbed 11 rebounds versus Miami. Mark Lyons was named Atlantic 10 Co-Rookie of the Week for the week ending Dec. 26. Lyons scored a career-high 13 points in the win over Miami while cracking into the starting lineup the last four games. Jordan Crawford led Xavier in scoring at 18.3 points per game, which ranked him third in the Atlantic 10 Conference.

Xavier's lone senior, Jason Love, led the team in rebounding at 9.7 rpg, putting him fourth in the Atlantic 10. Love grabbed a career-high 19 rebounds in the Cincinnati win, matching his 19-rebound effort from the Marquette game. Collectively the team was playing well, with the opening of conference play right around the corner.

A lot had been written about the game Xavier and Wake Forest were about to play, and that spoke volumes to the kind person Skip

Prosser was. Both athletic directors, Ron Wellman from Wake Forest and Mike Bobinski from Xavier, helped prepare a video tribute to be shown before the game, as well as introducing members of Prosser's family.

Mack said that he had not given much thought to the magnitude of the game until the team bus pulled up to the hotel. "When we arrived I started to see a lot of old faces there to greet us. It was my first time back since leaving, and it felt weird to be back in those surroundings knowing that Coach Prosser was not there. That is when I knew the next day or so was going to be difficult."

On the evening before the game Mack and his staff had returned from the team's shoot around at Joel Coliseum, a few miles from the Marriott where the team was staying. As usual the team would have their film session hi-lighting player tendencies and game thoughts in a ballroom located within the hotel. Afterward the players were dismissed for the evening, but Mack and his staff had one more item on their agenda.

Because of the extenuating circumstances and the closeness of the two staffs, there was a small gathering of both groups on the top floor of the hotel. Mit Shah, a prominent Wake Forest booster, and close friend of Mack's, had made the arrangements and taken care of food and beverage for all. What could have been an awkward moment for close friends Dino Gaudio, now the head coach at Wake Forest, and Mack, not to mention several assistant coaches with close ties, soon turned into a Skip Prosser storytelling affair.

Mack's favorite Prosser story took place when Skip coached his first basketball game on the freshmen level at Linsley Institute, "I could never do it justice, but I was willing to try for everyone in the room," said Mack.

The story goes that Prosser's team was down 18-0 to start the game. At some point during a mad scramble for a loose ball one of the opponent's players managed to steal the ball around half-court, but then began to dribble towards the wrong basket. Prosser was sure his team was about to score their first points of the season, regardless of the fact that those points were going to come from someone on the other team. That was when Prosser noticed one of his own players running the opposing player down in an attempt to block his shot. As the two players collided a foul was called and the shot was missed.

Mack said to the group, "Coach P would always finish this story the same way, 'If you think that was chaotic, you should have seen the referees trying to figure out where to shoot the free throws!'" Laughing, Mack said, "That story is just classic Coach Prosser, just classic."

Later the next evening, Xavier and Wake Forest stood on opposite ends of the court lined up for a pre-game ceremony to commemorate Prosser. When the video tribute was over there was barely a dry eye in the house as the lights came back on. Mack felt it was something different for his players to see members of the coaching staff, including Mack, shedding tears that close to tipoff, but when the ball went up in the air it simply became about winning the game.

Xavier led most of the first half and went into the locker room with a two point lead, 43-41. "We took advantage of Wake's turnovers, scoring 12 points, which was huge for us. We shot terrible from the field, but were able to stay in the game with our free throw shooting and defense, which created turnovers. We also did a good job on the glass getting the rebounding advantage 26-16," said Mack at the half.

The lead seesawed back and forth for most of the second half which sent the game down to the wire. Xavier had the ball at the end of regulation with 11.9 remaining and got the ball to Jordan Crawford who air-balled a heavily contested 3-pointer that Wake Forest's Chas McFarland caught with 2 seconds left. McFarland heaved the ball to the other end of the court in a desperation shot that fell short.

With under a minute to go in overtime Jamel McLean made a layup, and later a free throw, to give Xavier a three point lead. Then with 26 seconds to go Ishmael Smith from Wake Forest hit a three pointer to once again tie things up. Xavier, as they did at the end of regulation, had the ball for the last possession, but Terrell Holloway's shot was blocked as he drove the lane.

Second overtime.

Mack spoke about those two possessions after the game, "Well, I thought we could have gotten a better shot at the end of regulation.

Jordan took a jump shot that was contested and blocked. Both final shots were blocked – one going to the rim and one pulled up. But we wouldn't have been in the situation that we were to win the game if it wasn't for (Crawford). He made some terrific shots down the stretch. Because he had done that I wanted to put the ball in his hands. If I had to do it all over again, I would have really stressed to him, 'Get to the rim.' But he makes that shot in practice. And then I thought Holloway did what I asked and got to the basket and McFarland made one heck of a block to send the game into double overtime."

Xavier missed five shots in the last 1:27 of the second overtime. Crawford put up the team's last attempt with 1 second left and Al-Farouq Aminu rebounded the miss to preserve the win for the Demon Deacons.

"We knew that Aminu was going to be tough to stop, and we didn't stop him, he scored 26 points. What really got us, though, was the play of Ishmael Smith, a 17% shooter beyond the three point line, and he goes 3-3 from out there and scores 28 points. He was the difference in the game ultimately," said Mack in the aftermath of the loss.

Crawford was huge for Xavier scoring 30 points, often making shots to keep Xavier in the game. Jamel McLean also continued to come out of his funk to contribute heavily with 21 points, while leading the team with 10 rebounds.

As the players boarded their plane everyone looked exhausted. It was an emotional evening on a lot of levels, from the pre-game memorial for Prosser to the draining double overtime. Xavier's record sat at 8-5. Things would only become more difficult; later in the week Xavier would begin their rigorous 16 game conference schedule.

Since the calendar had now turned to 2010, talk would start to pick up about positions and seeding for the NCAA Tournament. If Xavier could post a decent conference record, somewhere around 12-4, they would be 20-9 overall, meaning the Florida game in about a month loomed large.

Xavier had pulled through probably the hardest part of their regular season schedule in decent shape, but a few opportunities, like Butler and Wake Forest, still lingered. "My biggest concern at that point was that we had not won a game on an opponent's home floor yet, and we had two tough games coming up in the next week to open conference play," said Mack.

Chapter 7

Second Season

Having returned four starters, and most of its scoring output from a team that had made it into the second round of the NCAA Tournament the prior year, the Dayton Flyers were the top choice of both coaches and selected media when the Atlantic 10 released its pre-season rankings. Xavier was a close second choice and were looking to become the first A-10 program to win four consecutive regular season titles since Massachusetts captured five straight from 1992-96.

Richmond, who had all five starters returning, was the choice for third, followed by LaSalle and Temple to round out the top five. Bringing up the bottom half of the conference were Charlotte, Rhode Island, Massachusetts, St. Joseph's, St. Bonaventure, Saint Louis, George Washington, and Fordham.

Mack knew from prior experience that these types of rankings held little value once the season started, "Believe me, we won't take anyone lightly because of their ranking. You also have to remember that none of us start playing each other until January. You'll be surprised by how different some of teams are playing according to their pre-season pick by then."

Mack had been right, by the time conference play began, teams picked for the lower half had been playing well. Temple had cracked into the bottom half of the Top 25, and Charlotte looked as though they were going to continue their strong start and contend for the regular season title until the end.

Before their first conference game against LaSalle, Xavier received some bad news on the injury front; Mark Lyons had suffered a severe bone bruise in his left knee during the Wake Forest game and would miss the next two games.

Lyons was proving to be an integral part of the team, fourth on the team in scoring at 9.4 points per game, and had 10.2 points as a starter in the last five games. Lyons sustained an injury during the first half of the Wake game, but was able to start the second half and played 20 total minutes. That meant a slight change in personnel for Xavier on the floor; Junior Dante Jackson would be slotted in as the back-up point guard while Lyons healed. Mack spoke about Jackson's ability to make the transition, "Dante hasn't always played his best at times this season but there's so much on his plate. I think he's more than capable of really filling in and it's a position I think he enjoys playing."

When the conference schedule opened up on the road against LaSalle, it wasn't pretty, but in the end Xavier was able to hold on and post a 68-62 victory. Jordan Crawford led all scorers with 22 points, and senior Jason Love posted 11 points and eight rebounds in his hometown. Xavier led by as much as 20 in the second half, but La Salle used a 20-0 run in the middle of the second half to tie the score.

La Salle's Kimmani Barrett cut the Xavier lead to six with a long 2-point jumper with 8:19 left in the game. Then LaSalle's Rodney Green knotted the game at 56 with a layup at the 4:04 mark. Xavier took its final lead of the game with 2:18 left when Dante Jackson hit a 3-pointer to give the Musketeers a 63-60 lead. Jackson finished the game with nine points on 3-of-5 shooting from behind the arch.

Mack spoke of his team's effort afterwards, "It wasn't the prettiest win in the world, but we found a way to get out of there with a win and fortunately start the conference season 1-0."

The team quickly made its way to Washington D.C. that Thursday evening and would have some time off until their next game against George Washington in three days. The break was a bit unusual, but there was a reason which Mack explained, "We felt it made more sense for us to stay out on the road and sort of hole up and really get focused to try and get off to a 2-0 start. We normally would have come home, but it would have just been for one day and then back out, so in the end it made more sense to just go direct from one game to the next."

The night before the George Washington game Mack received what he has often said is his worst fear, a middle of the night call from the hotel staff regarding one of his players. The call had come from the lobby. Mack was told that someone from his program was quite inebriated and had been picked up by the police outside of the hotel.

A sleepy eyed Mack tried to sort through the scenarios he was going to encounter when he got downstairs, none of them good. "I would have to say that my biggest fear is that at any time I could get that phone call that tells me one of my players has made a bad decision. These are college age kids after all, and you just never know what they might get themselves into. We try and instruct them in ways in which to make the best choices, but they are out of our sight a lot of the time while they are here in school, and that can allow for bad things to happen."

To Mack's relief, and somewhat amusement, the person in question was someone that used to have ties to the program, but was now working at another school. He had been picked up by the police on the street, and when they asked him what hotel he was staying at, he by chance happened to give the one where Xavier was. The front desk staff, knowing that Xavier was the only team staying with them, assumed the person was part of the Xavier travel party. Luckily in the end he wasn't.

"It ended up being a relief, but being awoken like that in the middle of the night meant I did not have much luck getting back to sleep. Now that part was not funny," said Mack.

Mack was able to keep himself awake the next day as Xavier recorded a 76-69 come-from-behind victory at George Washington in a game that was a tale of two halves.

The Colonials led 41-30 at halftime in large part because of 11 Xavier first half turnovers, a 14-9 rebounding advantage, and 59.3 percentage in shooting from the field.

Xavier reversed the trend in all three areas the second half, outscoring GW 46-28. Xavier handled the ball much better, committing only three turnovers, controlled the boards 30-19, and lastly, held the Colonials to 31.0 percent shooting from the field.

"It was real simple at the half; we told them to keep their hands on the ball and go get more rebounds. If they did those two things they would be 2-0," Mack explained.

Xavier still trailed by 10 points, 60-50, with less than eight minutes left in the game.

That's when the Musketeers put together a 20-1 run over the next seven minutes to take control of the game at 70-61 with 41 seconds remaining. Senior Jason Love led Xavier in scoring (19) and rebounding (13), including 12 points and 12 rebounds in the second half alone. That game marked the fifth double-double of the season for Love.

Sophomore Jordan Crawford, quickly making a name for himself around the conference, scored 18 points, including 13 in the second half, while sophomore Terrell Holloway scored 14 of his 15 points in the second half. Holloway, who was still leading the Atlantic 10 in free throw shooting, hit 13 of his 14 free throws attempts to help seal the win down the stretch.

"Again, we're excited to get out of there with a win and be 2-0. We knew though, that we couldn't keep putting ourselves in those types of situations as we had in that first week of conference play and expect to win consistently," Mack said in the aftermath of the opening road trip.

Two days later the team jumped in deep preparing for their next foe Charlotte. Mack addressed everyone at midcourt before practice commenced and said, "Charlotte is very talented, but if you continue to hammer them for 40 minutes they will break, that is who they are. They broke the other night with a few minutes to go, and in some of their other games we have seen them pack it in and play zone. Give me a good hour and a half, yesterday was mental, today is physical, let's go."

Mack made his rounds passing by each position group, making certain points along the way. With the guards Mack stressed to the players, "Charlotte is a team that will shoot a bunch in transition, be prepared for them to pull up, you have to defend that. When they get into their half court offense they will set a bunch of ball screens, we need you to whip though those hard, with high hands."

With the big men Mack instructed how he wanted them to defend Charlotte's Shamari Spears, "Spears will fade away over his right shoulder, or crow hop into the middle and baby hook. Make sure you crowd him the whole time."

To the team as a whole, "Charlotte runs a lot of set plays, like a football team. If they don't work they pull the ball back out and start over. No better way to monkey their game plan up than to provide ball pressure at all times. They will turn the ball over."

The team finished practice defending some of Charlotte's weave with double screens in the lane. Mack assessed the team's chances, "I think if we can be super physical on defense we'll be ok. I think the team is starting to find an identity and would like to make a statement with this game after opening the conference with two close ones."

The team was focused as they assembled in the locker room for last minute instructions before taking the floor for their first home conference game. Mack pointed to the board behind him, "Ok, as we always stress, tonight's game is ten four-minute wars. Let's focus on the war we are in and not get ahead of ourselves. 7 kills on defense, if we can do that we'll win. We had five kills at the half against LaSalle, which created a lot of separation, which, as you know, we needed later in the game.

"Fellas I want you to remember tonight that this is our house. When I am at home and hear something downstairs in the middle of the night I come running down with a butcher knife. I want you to have that same mentality. Last year, when we lost down there, Charlotte was yelling and carrying on out in the hallway near our locker room. We didn't like that, so I want you to return that favor to them tonight."

Xavier got off to a decent start winning the first two wars 11-5 and 10-6 to build a comfortable ten point lead. The big men were doing their part on defense and crowding Spears as instructed, making him a non-factor to that point in the game. Spears' frustration led to his second foul with eight minutes to go in the half.

As the team came into the timeout Mack yelled over the crowd, "Listen, that's two on Spears, they have some serious foul trouble on the interior, so let's start working the ball down low to Love and

Frease." The team listened, and went into the half having built a six-teen point lead 44-28.

Mack and the staff liked the effort they had seen so far and had only a short list of directives for the second half. Mack delivered these quickly before the team headed back out to the floor, "Guys let's have a share-the-ball mentality this half. Move the ball around and create opportunities on the perimeter and down low. We can't let off the pace; we need to keep running the ball up the court. On defense watch Spears. He will be trying to go to the crow hop this half since we took away his fade away in the first.

"Lastly fellas, Charlotte is only in this game for one reason; re-bounding. If we were doing what we needed to on the glass we would be up by thirty. Charlotte will go down and post a mismatch if they get one, so make sure you talk. Championship teams do not take their foot off the pedal."

Charlotte cut the lead to 65-50 when Dante Jackson fouled out midway through the second half. Mack felt things beginning to get a bit tenuous, so he made sure to get his team's attention during the next timeout, "Guys if we really stay focused on the next four min-utes we can end this thing. Keep your focus and execute like we did in the first half."

Charlotte would actually cut the lead to ten points during that next four minute stretch, but would get no closer. Xavier clamped down on the defensive end to finally hold off the 49'ers and get the win 86-74. Mack addressed a jubilant team afterward in their locker room, "Fellas, great win over a very talented team. I was a bit dis-appointed how we did around the basket in the 2nd half, so we need to work on that the next few days. We had some high notes, 18 as-sists, and we were solid from beyond the three point line. Frease and Love had no turnovers, great job.

"Guys listen; next we have Dayton who was pre-season number #1 in the A-10. Every damn paper this summer talked about Dayton, whether it was ESPN, Sporting News, or Andy Katz; when it came to the A-10 it was all about Dayton. I'm sick of hearing about Dayton being the top team in our conference; I want to see us change that this weekend. Last time I checked I didn't see any A-10 banners hanging in their joint.

"There is a lot that we will need to do in order to win, Dayton is a good team, don't get me wrong. We need to guard them in transition since they are a team that prides themselves on getting up the floor and rebounding. But remember this, right now we are first in conference, and that will not change come Saturday."

The Dayton game presented a unique challenge with an 11 a.m. starting time to accommodate scheduling the game which was going to be nationally televised on ESPN2. Even with the odd start time the team was still focused and ready come tipoff.

The first half was a tense, taut affair that saw numerous ties and lead changes throughout that left Xavier with a three point deficit at the half 39-36. Dayton's defense had shut down Jordan Crawford in the first half holding to him to just two points.

The second half, however, was a different story with Crawford coming out and shooting a trey to tie the score. Dayton kept it close though, coming as close as three in the final minute of play, but Xavier held on and prevailed for the win 78-74. Danté Jackson scored a career high 19 points and was the game's leading scorer which served as the energizing boost Xavier needed down the stretch. Mack had high praise for Jackson afterward, "He was incredible in the first half. When he is shooting the ball the way he was, how can you say 'stop shooting'? He is the emotional sparkplug of our team. His heart is in the right place. He loves his team. He loves this program."

Mack was upbeat after netting another big win at home over one of the better teams in the conference, "The effort of both teams was incredible. Give Dayton a lot of credit. They annihilated us on the offensive glass. They are really good. In the second half we settled down on offense, which I attribute to the message we gave at the half; getting the ball inside."

The game came down to rebounding and free throws. Dayton dominated Xavier on the boards by a mark of 51 to 34, but Xavier scored when it counted from the free throw line shooting 80 percent on 24 of 30 attempts. Dayton, comparatively, was 64 percent on 16 of 25. Sophomore Jordan Crawford exploded for 14 of his 16 points in the second half, while Terrell Holloway added 17 points, and once again, going nearly perfect from the line, 13-for-14. Senior captain Jason Love scored 10 points and had a career high six blocks.

Earlier in the week the team had received news that Mark Lyons had healed and would be available to play in the Dayton game, which he did, logging 13 minutes. Mack spoke about Lyon's effort, "Cheeks did a really good job today. He would have liked to play 40 minutes, but we need to ease him back into things. He's anxious to play, and we wouldn't allow him to play if we felt like it was the wrong decision. We'll certainly need his contributions during the remainder of the season."

Even though Xavier was working their way through the conference schedule nicely to that point, the intensity at the team's last practice before the Temple game would have given no indication to that fact. Mack and his staff were working the players hard the entire time they were on the floor. Mack, as usual, was making the rounds, barking out instructions to all, but had some pointed comments to a few.

To Brad Redford, Mack harped on getting sloppy and turning the ball over, "Brad, against Temple we need possessions, you have to be smart when you have the ball, and work harder to get open when you don't." To big man Kenny Frease, "Kenny, you have to get your feet set and be strong going to the rim." Mack didn't like what he was seeing effort-wise from the whole team, especially Jamel McLean, "C'mon Jamel, what are you doing out there? Every now and then you get that look in your eye that tells me you want to play, then you come out here and loaf around and get burned on D. How much do you really want to play? Mel, you gotta be an athletic defender, someone who gives a damn on defense."

Mack continued on that point to the entire group, "Fellas, if we get lazy on defense it leads to dumb fouls. A key point in this next game is this, we shoot 80% from the free throw line and are 2nd in the conference, Temple is first. Don't give them the opportunity to go to the line more than they need to. We have to concentrate on what we are doing at all times."

Mack had told his players at the close of practice that in order to win they had to accomplish three things, "Pressure the ball, set the pace because they will give easy baskets in transition, and third, pound it in and score down low. If we can do well at those three things we stand a good chance of winning tomorrow night."

Xavier did win the rebounding battle, but fell short when it came to giving up points in transition and scoring down on the block, which led to a loss to Temple 77-72. Mack was prescient when he warned the team about Temple's proficiency at the line as the Owls made clutch free throws, one after another, down the stretch. The Musketeers made things interesting in the final minute, by shaving into the Temple lead. Brad Redford hit a 3-pointer from the wing with 55 seconds left in the game to cut the score to 70-65 in favor of Temple. Redford struck again at the 23.4 mark with a three from the corner that brought Xavier to within three, 71-68, but that was as close as they would get.

Mack was a bit down afterward, having just lost their first conference game of the year. "While we were disappointed with how we played and how we performed on the defensive end, I'm not going to cash in our chips and say we're done. I mean, you've got to move forward. You've got to be able to correct the mistakes you made, and that's how a team progresses throughout the year. Temple sure made it tough on us; they shot nearly 60% from the field. But we still have to find a way to get it done"

Mack though continued to think big picture, "You just have to improve. The naysayers will talk about our defense, our offense, our this and that. We know what we have to improve on, and we can't lose our mind based on one game. But we know we're more than capable. If we're locked in, and we're who we need to be, then we can contend for the championship."

Perhaps a renewed focus for the next home game three nights later against Rhode Island was why Mack was getting on Kenny Frease an hour before game time, "Kenny I heard you were late getting here is that true?"

"No, Coach," replied Frease.

"If I find out different you're not starting," Mack said to Frease, then turned and announced to the group as a whole, "C'mon fellas, this is a big game tonight at the Cintas Center, no loafing around. I don't like what I'm seeing, let's get focused!" Mack let the room sit silent for a minute then asked assistant Travis Steele to go over personnel for Rhode Island.

For each game, part of the preparation for the assistants is to go over each player on the opposing team they think will, or might, see time on the floor. On a rotating basis, Steele and Kelsey were assigned the advance scouting responsibilities of upcoming opponents. A comprehensive report detailing each player's tendencies, strengths, and weaknesses would be handed out to the players prior to game day. That same information was copied onto poster board sheets that Steele was now walking the team through. This ritual always occurred just under an hour before tipoff.

When Steele was done Mack walked to the front of the room to summarize, "Let's take care of the ball out there and limit turnovers. We don't want to see more than 12 tonight. Let's have effort and urgency in the half-court when we run our offense. Rhode Island has no real solid system on defense to defend how we want to move the ball.

"On defense remember that Rhode Island sets plays to drive the ball, let's wall up hard, take charges, and get the rebound. They do an average job of blocking out."

The meeting ended with the team filing out of the room past Mack and down the hallway for stretching in the weight room prior to their first shoot around.

It is during this time that Mack will quietly pace back and forth in the locker room, alone, giving thought to specific points he wants up on the board for his pre-game talk.

Mack says of the routine, "I rarely know ahead of time what I want to say, so I do like to take those couple of quiet minutes to try and summarize some of my general thoughts on the game ahead. The message can often change depending on the opponent, the time of year, and where the team's mindset is in general."

For Rhode Island the dry erase board read: Win the War We Are In – proven in 17/18 games win or lose; Energy! You? – Be a team of Energizer Bunnies, play your hardest; Tough Minded and Fearless – complete every possession.

"I wanted to stress to the team that we took plays off at Temple and it led to a loss. The best teams do not do that, and I warned them that if I saw them doing that they were coming out of the game," said Mack.

Despite the warning Xavier came out flat against Rhode Island. Sloppy ball handling led to a three point deficit at the half. What had really bothered Mack though, was the team had only scored 26 points. This had Mack at his most animated to that point in the season when he addressed the team, "What the hell are we doing out here? We talked about 12 turnovers for the game; we had 12 in the first half! Mark Lyons, get your head in the game. You're making 40-foot entry passes into the post. It's playground ball, let's go!

"On offense we play like we have no plan. Do we even watch film? I'm seeing nothing out there. Do what we do in practice; it's a matter of us being lazy with the ball. You are lucky to only be down three. In the second half get the damn ball inside, Love has no points, get him the ball! If he becomes a pig with it, I'll handle that."

Mack stormed out of the locker room hoping to have inspired the troops. Mack's fiery temper almost led to his first technical of the year when a blocking call went against Xavier in front of their own bench. The ball had come into Mack's hands, who looked as though he was about to throw it back to the referee while ranting about the call. Mario Mercurio had to step in and restrain Mack.

Xavier later battled through the adversity when Kenny Frease was called with two quick fouls and was out of the game with eleven minutes to go. The foul call ignited Xavier, who rallied and started to convert on offense. Xavier also upped the intensity on the defensive end and started to wear Rhode Island down.

Xavier, behind a collective team effort, finally pulled clear, putting away the Rams 72-61. Jordan Crawford had his first career double-double with 21 points and 12 rebounds. Crawford additionally dished out six assists, and had two clutch three-pointers to tie the game and give Xavier the lead to start the second half.

Jamel McLean had an outstanding game, providing a spark off the bench scoring 16 points while grabbing eight rebounds. Terrell Holloway was Mr. Consistent from the line, again, going 6-of-7, scoring a total of 12 points to go along with four assists. Senior Jason Love contributed 10 points to the affair along with six rebounds.

Mack addressed the team afterward in a much different mood

than at halftime, "Fellas I'm proud of this team. We held a team that averaged 80 points to 60. They shot 40% from the field and 13% from the3-point line. There was a lot that we didn't do right tonight; 18 turnovers and an off night shooting, but you proved tonight that when we do what we do, play tough-nosed defense, it can make up for a lot."

Later, upstairs in his office, Mack took a deep breath, knowing his team may have gotten away with one earlier in the evening, "We beat an excellent team. I have a lot of respect for the University of Rhode Island. Coach Baron does a great job. The difference was we did a great job defensively. You have to learn how to finish a game with a young team. I'm proud of our team.

"I thought in the first half we were nonchalant with the basketball, not meeting passes. We got better at that and had only six turnovers in the second half, we scored 46 points and put the game away."

Mack spoke of Jordan Crawford's continuing excellence as the team leader on offense as the season progressed, "When he lets the game come to him, he's a dominant player. I was really happy with how he rebounded the ball – 12 rebounds. He changed the game entirely. To have six assists and 12 rebounds, I thought his performance was great."

Mack felt the game served another purpose, "It got their attention. When a team wins they have a tendency to get complacent, when they lose, or have to work really hard for a win, like we did tonight, you sort of have their undivided attention again."

The team had a laser-like focus after the Rhode Island game, and wanted to send a message to the rest of the conference that they were going to be very difficult to handle the remainder of the year. That message was delivered loud and clear by winning the next two games over Duquesne and Fordham by 36 and 48 points respectively.

Mack's pregame Duquesne speech spoke right to the heart of the matter; to get it going right from the opening tip. Xavier had lost the first two four-minute wars against Rhode Island, and Mack didn't want a replay of that same scenario against Duquesne. To further illustrate his point Mack told a story about an old Cincinnati icon.

"Any of you guys ever heard of Aaron Pryor. No? YouTube him then, he was a tough nosed middleweight fighter that grew up about five miles from here. Pryor's style was when the bell rang he ran right across the ring and started throwing haymakers against his opponent. Boom! Boom! Boom! One after another, and most of the time he won his fights within the first two rounds.

"When Pryor fought Alexis Arguello, the reigning middleweight champion, who was considered a much better fighter than Pryor, many people expected that Pryor would change his style, but he didn't. When the bell rang against Arguello, Pryor did the same thing; Boom! Boom! Boom!"

Mack said to the team, "Tonight I want you guys to have that same attitude against Duquesne. I don't want us to feel our way into the game. I want haymakers from the opening tip, now let's go!"

The team got the message and came out swinging, leading by 20 at the half and never looking back. Against Fordham three nights later it was more of the same, a 45-32 lead at the half after never trailing, then pouring it on in the second half 63-28.

Xavier, now rolling, was halfway through the conference schedule with a record of 7-1. Good enough to hold a one game lead over Charlotte and Temple, who were both 6-1. Mack commented on the team's performance to that point in the season, "So far we like what we see. Of course, we are always looking for ways to get better. My main concern right now has been turnovers. We have had quite a few lately; we need to do a better job of handling the ball."

Xavier began the latter part of their conference schedule with a road trip to face UMASS. After getting out to a 15 point lead at the half Xavier again found themselves in a closely contested game as the second unfolded.

A late second-half 16-4 run by Massachusetts gave the Minutemen their first lead, 63-62. The two squads traded buckets, and the lead until back-to-back three-pointers from Crawford, and an old-fashioned three-point play by McLean which gave Xavier the advantage back for good at 77-69. Xavier would win in the end 87-79.

Afterward Mack lamented on the teams recurring turnover problems, "I would say my biggest concern is just the lackadaisical first four to six minutes of the second half because when you do that on the road, usually you get beat. It was a repeat performance that we had against La Salle. It was too easy too early, we were playing well, and the other team really decided to become aggressive. We were on our heels, and not just on turnovers, overall it was just how we played on both ends of the floor coming out of halftime. That was disappointing."

Despite some of the team's shortcomings, Mack also saw some positives in Jamel McLean's performance. McLean had cracked back into the starting lineup a few games earlier against Duquesne and had continued to play well finishing with 14 points and 11 rebounds, "He's playing a lot better. He got another double-double. I think he would have had about 20 points if he converted some of those drop offs early in the first half."

But always the coach, Mack couldn't resist to point out an area that needed some attention from McLean, "The one thing that Jamel isn't comfortable with yet is that left hand. Sometimes he goes chest-to-chest with his defender. He draws the foul but he can't get the shot off. In a couple instances they were blocked shots, they went the other way. He's got to be able to utilize his off hand and shield the defender, and when he does that he can become a special player."

Even with the satisfaction of a road win over a conference opponent there was never time to rest. The UMASS game represented the first of three huge road games over a ten day period, with Dayton and Florida to follow.

Xavier was now 16-6 overall and 8-1 in the conference, while continuing to have both a strong RPI rating and strength of schedule. Numbers that would be critically important come NCAA Selection Sunday, which was still a little more than a month away.

Chapter 8

Stretch Run

Cincinnati had been hit with a snowstorm the evening before the Dayton game, meaning the team decided to stay closer to the arena than normal. Maybe the change in plans was a precursor of things to come as Xavier was hit with a storm of their own the next day by their opponent the Dayton Flyers.

Less than two minutes into the game Jason Love had drawn his second foul essentially taking him out of the game before anyone even broke a sweat. Mack looked on in disbelief at the referees who naturally had little consolation. Mack looked at his dad, Tom, who was sitting in the first row behind the bench as if to say, 'this really can't be happening, are you kidding me?'

Dayton came into the game needing a win over Xavier in a big way to get back into the conference race, and perhaps buoyed by the calls against Xavier, retained control the rest of the way to lead by 13 at the half. Xavier cut the lead to 10 at one point in the second half, but got no closer, and lost by a huge margin, 90-65.

Xavier was not only outscored by a wide margin, they got hammered on the boards and shot terribly from the field. Adding insult to injury, Charlotte beat Fordham that same day to garner the top spot in conference standings with an 8-1 record, Xavier had fallen a half-game behind to 8-2. Third place was a three way tie between No. 19 ranked Temple, Richmond and Rhode Island.

Maybe, in retrospect, the Dayton loss was the best thing that could have happened to Xavier. With an entire week open before their road game in Florida it gave the team a chance to get back home, lick their wounds, and get focused and prepared for their biggest out-of-conference game on the schedule. Florida in recent years had become a powerhouse program under the guidance of Billy Donovan. Donovan, who played at Providence under Rick Pitino, led the Friars to a Final Four appearance in 1987, and was later an assistant under Pitino at Kentucky. Donovan was at Marshall University for a brief stint, successfully turning that program around before taking the Florida job in 1996. Four years later Donovan had guided the Gators to the National Championship game in Indianapolis, eventually losing to Tom Izzo and Michigan State.

That run, however, laid the foundation for future success that saw Florida win it all with back to back national titles in 2006 and 2007. The 2009-2010 version of the program was not as dominant, with a 17-7 record, and just 6-4 in the conference at the time of the game.

In the days leading up to the Florida matchup, Mack began using the term "Outside the Wire" with his players. As he huddled up the team during the morning shoot-around, Mack explained the definition. "It's a military term troops use when they are on foreign soil. If they're on base they know that, for the most part, they're safe. Certainly things can go wrong, but generally when you are at home base it's business as usual. When you step off that base, however, and go 'outside the wire' (the military fencing separating the base from the outside world) you had better be alert at all times, in all directions. A mistake 'outside the wire' could cost you your life."

Mack wanted to use this term to explain to his team that they were at Florida as the visiting team and he wanted to see a hardened mentality. Mack wanted every player who checked in to the game to be alert, ready to go, and execute. No excuses would be allowed.

The players got the message, and when the game started Xavier pushed out to a 16 point lead during the first half, but Florida chipped away, cutting the lead to seven at the half. "At the break we stressed continuing to protect the ball, turnovers had been a problem recently, and we were getting better, but the point still needed to be made. We also talked about getting the ball inside to Love and McLean. We felt as though we could get some good matchups in our favor and we wanted to make that a point of emphasis in the second half," said Mack as he worked his way from the locker room back to the court.

"We also knew that we had let Florida back in the game, and again we wanted to see the kids come out with an aggressive and fearless style of play at the beginning of the second half. We had lost the last two wars to close out the first half, and we had talked in the past about the importance of the first four minutes of the next half."

Despite setting the tone early in the second half, Xavier finally saw their entire lead evaporate when Florida went up by two with 10 minutes to go in the game. Xavier fought back, reeling off seven unanswered points; punctuated by a Dante Jackson three point shot and a Kenny Frease dunk just before the 8 minute TV timeout. From there, Xavier was able to hang on down the stretch for the win 76-64.

Mack said in the aftermath, "I'm really proud of the guys after tonight's effort. We played an extremely talented and well coached team that was not going to back down. We got in some tight spots, but fought back and found a way to get it done. I was especially impressed by the fact that we were able to make adjustments at both ends of the floor throughout the game, that's the sign of a special team."

Mack concluded, "I think a lot of the fan base had this game circled on their calendar. I think it sends a strong message to a national audience that watched the game on ESPN that Xavier can play with anyone and that we'll be a tough team come tournament time." Xavier was led by senior Jason Love who finished the game with 20 points and 10 rebounds. Love's effort won him co-title as the Atlantic 10 Player of the Week announced the following Tuesday.

There was a new leader atop the A-10 standings with Richmond having moved ahead of Xavier, Charlotte, and Temple. The Spiders had posted a 9-2 record that also saw them crack into the 25th position in the national rankings. Temple was also ranked at 21st. After the Florida win Xavier stood at 20th in the RPI rankings, and 14th in strength of schedule. Now that the team had passed the test down in Florida it was starting to look like making the NCAA Tournament was well within reach.

The team would be off Sunday to enjoy their big road win, but for Mack, there is no such thing as a day off, as Mack's schedule would attest. The next morning Mack was up early on his way to Lunken Airport to meet associate head coach Pat Kelsey. Mack and Kelsey were going to spend the day visiting Jay Canty, one of the four players that had signed a letter of intent back in November to attend Xavier.

Kelsey was accompanying Mack because he had built the relationship with Canty during the recruitment period. It was Kelsey that had first contact with Canty who was a native of High Point, North Carolina. Canty had warmed up to Kelsey right away, having previously known Kelsey from his time at Wake Forest.

The trip started when the two boarded a private plane at Lunken, within minutes they were up above the clouds talking about some of the players they were recruiting, the win last night over Florida, and sharing ideas regarding the next few opponents on the schedule. Two hours later the plane touched down in New Jersey where Mack and Kelsey piled into a waiting rental car and made their way to Sovereign Bank Arena where Canty was playing in a prep school tournament. Mack pointed out that even though they already had a commitment from Canty, the trip was an important one, "Trips like this are vital because they serve as an extension of what you said to a player when you were originally recruiting him.

"When we told Jay that we wanted him to come to Xavier, and that we were committed to his development as a person and a player, we meant it. By showing up from time to time to see how he is playing and progressing speaks to that point."

Mack feels that if you work hard to recruit someone to come join your program, then they sign, and don't hear or see you until they set foot on campus, it sends a mixed message. As Mack pointed out, "What's a kid supposed to think when you are there 24/7 during the recruiting period, and then after he signs, nothing? I just feel it sets the wrong tone. We want Jay to know that even though he won't be on campus until later in the year, he is already part of the Xavier family."

When the games were complete Mack and Kelsey spent some time with Canty and his family then headed back to the airport. A short time later, after a quick stop at Five Guys and Fries, both coaches hopped back on the plane for the flight back home. It was another long day in a long season, but not one out of the ordinary.

Fans only see a small portion of what goes into coaching at this level. It's trips like the one that Mack and Kelsey took, a day after beating Florida and on a Sunday, which meant another day away from their family. It's part of what makes the job so demanding.

Mack talked about the toll the job can take on the home life, "I'm no different than anyone else, I love to spend time with my wife and kids, especially on the weekend, but the many demands on my time are endless, and can be difficult. But you know what you're getting into, and it just sort of becomes part of the overall picture. I don't think any of us could be successful doing our jobs if we didn't have someone rock solid on the home front."

"For me, my wife Christi has been a tremendous source of support in years past, and even more so this year. When I was offered the head coaching position, the decision to accept was a joint one because it takes the two of us, working together, to make it happen."

Mack does what he can to support Christi in her own endeavors when he gets the time. As the head women's basketball coach at Colerain High School, Christi had her own team and schedule that demanded a great deal of her time during Mack's first season. Christi's team did well in her final season as the coach, finishing with a 17-5 record before bowing out in the state sectional finals. It was to be her final year on the sidelines, since she wanted to devote more time to the family and girls in the future.

After getting back from his recruiting trip to the East coast Mack was able to devote some time to his family before taking on St. Joseph's the next evening. Christi's Colerain team had a game against Sycamore High School, so Mack would be in the stands with the roles reversed; he was now spectator and babysitter while his wife stalked the sidelines.

Mack spoke quickly as he juggled both Lainee, 4, and Hailee, 3, "I'm like any other dad in the stands tonight. I won't see much of the game, because I am busy trying to keep the girls occupied, and of course, any minute now they're going to be hungry. That's when the fun really begins."

Mack has gotten used to the interruptions when in public with his family. Many attending the game had noticed Mack there with his girls, and at halftime a few fans made their way over to ask for an autograph or a picture. Mack obliged every one, "I feel it's the right thing to do, and the fans are respectful when I am with family. I like to talk to people and see what they have to say, I like mingling with our fan base, it's a fun part of the job. Our fans are so passionate and supportive of our program, so I think to take a minute or two and talk to them about Xavier basketball is part of what I'm paid to do."

When the game was over, Mack told Christi that he would take the girls to Skyline Chili for dinner before heading home. After a fair amount of noodles, cheese, and crackers had been consumed it was time to go home and get the girls to bed. After the girls were down Mack was able to unwind with Christ for awhile, rehashing the past few days, and talking a bit about Christi's game earlier that evening. Mack ended the night switching back and forth between a few college games on television.

Thus far in the season the pace had been breakneck for Mack, Christi said, "I didn't think that going into the season Chris could work more than he did, but I was wrong. Knowing that he has the responsibility for the entire program means that the job never stops for Chris."

Because of the demands of Mack's schedule and the impact it has on his family, Christi had made the decision at year end to stop coaching her Colerain team, she said, "Even though it was a tough decision I had to do it for my family. I wanted to be able to say in the future that 'I really missed coaching' and not 'I sure missed raising my kids.'

"In a way I won't miss the game as much because with Chris' job I am still pretty immersed in the game. I'm a basketball junkie, especially college basketball. I can still get my fix by spending time talking to Chris and watching film with him at home. I love going to the games and seeing the plays Chris has talked about unfold on the floor."

Christi is not your typical coaches' wife; sitting in the stands looking nervous anticipating what is to come next, "I feel pretty much at ease because the coach in me takes over. I'm watching the plays on the floor, looking to see players get in position, etc. With all of the time that I spend around Chris and seeing how confident he is in the team's preparation for each game, it helps put me at ease."

Christi feels that Mack had done an incredible job all year long keeping a pretty even keel himself, "I was amazed how well Chris kept his composure all year. Early in the season, when the team had lost to Butler, and many probably felt that the pressure was on, I didn't see any change in him. I think it just goes back to the fact that Chris had a system in place, and was confident that given time, things would start to fall into place. And they did as the season wore on."

After the Florida win a lot of talk began about the fact that Xavier would be a lock to make it into the NCAA Tournament. Mack would have none of it though, never looking any farther ahead than the next opponent on the schedule, which was back home at the Cintas Center against conference rival St. Joseph's. The team buckled down and got a relatively easy win by the final of 88-52.

Next was Charlotte; a team that had played well most of the year, but was starting to stumble a bit down the stretch. Despite the recent spate of poor play, Charlotte was still a dangerous opponent, especially on their home court. The team was well aware of this, but Mack provided some added comedic incentive anyhow, "Fellas I want to tell you a quick story about Charlotte. Now, we all know that it's a big game for a lot of different reasons, but I also want to see us win it for a personal reason. Every year that we have been going down there since I came back to Xavier to coach under Coach Miller there is this guy that sits right behind our bench; you'll see him when we get there. He will ride us and heckle us the whole game, especially me. When I first went there this guy yells out to me before the tip, 'Hey Johnny Appleseed we're gonna kick your ass tonight!' So, starting with that game in particular, which we won, I have always made a point to make sure I get his attention and give him a little wink as we walk off the court after a win. Let's make sure that we keep that streak alive."

A few nights later, Xavier was able to do just that, and Mack was able to wink at his sideline friend after Xavier handled Charlotte convincingly 81-67.

The torrid recruiting pace continued for Mack after the Charlotte game. This time, as a midweek practice ended, the players weren't even to the locker room yet before Mack and assistant Travis Steele were heading over to Lunken Airport to catch a chartered flight to

Bloomington, Indiana. Mack, knowing that he couldn't comment on unsigned recruits, invited me to go along.

It was a big time high school matchup featuring Dee Davis, who had already committed to Xavier for the 2011 season, playing against Pike High School featuring Marques Teague. Teague, a junior like Davis, had been pursued by many programs, but ultimately settled on Kentucky. It was an exciting game, and the action did not disappoint. Both point guards played inspired basketball as the game seesawed back and forth throughout. When the game concluded Mack and Steele spent some time with J.R. Holmes, the head coach at Bloomington South, and the rest of their coaching staff. Afterwards, it was back to the plane for the return trip home. After dropping Steele off back at the Cintas Center Mack ran up to his office to grab some film before heading home. Mack started to preview some of the tapes he wanted to watch, and like so many other nights, he ended up staying much later than anticipated.

The overhead lights from Mack's office cascaded down into the upper deck of the empty Cintas Center. Mack was thinking out loud as he looked out his office window and said, "It's times like this when I can look out onto the court, when all is quiet and dark that I sometimes reflect on where I am. I really am truly blessed to have this opportunity, to coach here at Xavier, and lead this group of kids. Plus, I have such a great support system that enables me to do that."

After a short pause, Mack stood up and drew the blinds on his office window, shut down his computer and said, "Speaking of that support system, I think it's time I finally got home."

Next up on the schedule was a short trip over to St. Louis. Mack thought since it would be a quick trip, with just one overnight stay, it would be a good opportunity to take along his older daughter, "It was a great chance to bring Lainee along. We weren't going to be too far away from home, plus, Christi's parents, who live in Louisville, were going to come over for the game. Lainee, like all kids, loves to see her grandparents, so she was excited for the trip."

The team flew over to St. Louis the day before the game, and after landing, the team bus made its way over to the arena for a shootaround before heading to the team hotel. After dinner with the team Mack had to get Lainee up to the room for bedtime. All seemed to be going well until Mack closed the door to his suite only to turn around and see his daughter standing there starting to cry.

Mack said, "Everything went smooth until we got up to the room, that's when the fun was over for the day, she's tired as it is, then she starts to cry and say she wants to go home and that she misses mommy.

"At this point I'm thinking, uh-oh, this has taken a turn for the worse. I told her that everything was fine, she was with her Daddy and was going to see her Grandma and Grandpa tomorrow since Christi's parents were coming to the game." The promise of grandparents seemed to finally calm things down. So, after Lainee finally drifted off to sleep Mack spent some time going over St. Louis personnel one more time before turning in himself.

The next morning pancakes and chocolate milk were on the menu for Mack and his daughter before the team headed over to the arena for their pregame shoot-around. As the team filed out onto the court Mack still had Lainee at his side, and needed to find something for her to do so he could go out onto the court and go over a few things with the players.

While Mack was looking around deciding what to do with Lainee, Mario Mercurio came to the rescue and told Mack to go, he would watch Lainee. Mack was able to tend to his duties, while Mercurio kept Lainee occupied coloring at the scorer's table for the next hour. As Mercurio played the role of pseudo dad he looked up and quipped, "Whatever it takes."

Xavier continued their winning ways later that evening with another well played road win over a surprising St. Louis team 73-71. St. Louis had been picked to finish 12th in the pre-season conference poll, but under the guidance of veteran coach Rick Majerus, the Billikens had come together nicely as the season progressed.

The win over St. Louis cleared the way for a big home showdown against Richmond, now ranked in the Top 25. Xavier, Richmond, and Temple were all tied for the conference lead, so Xavier, for all intents and purposes, could eliminate Richmond from the regular season championship with a win during a game which was going to be nationally televised on ESPN2.

For Mack and Xavier, a win over Richmond would probably get

them into the Top 25, and thus improve their seeding in the upcoming NCAA Tournament. Additionally, Xavier had plenty of big wins on their resume, and it appeared that just about every team they had lost to was moving on to the postseason as well. In many circles Xavier was being projected as a #6 or #7 seed in the field of 64.

While Mack was well aware of what may lie ahead for the team, he was talking about nothing but what Xavier needed to do in order to beat Richmond the afternoon of the game.

Mack made some last minute notes on the board and turned to face the team, "Guys I say it every game, ten four-minute wars. Be greedy, win them all. If we happen to lose one let's figure out what we need to do to win the next one. I don't want you to think of it as a big forty minute game, just focus on what you need to do in the next four minutes.

"640 down to 120. We talked back before the LaSalle game that we had 640 minutes to win the A-10 regular season title; we're now down to three games. Most of the teams in this league cannot catch us at this point, but the team that is about 100 yards down the hall can."

Mack continued, "You guys are a skilled and special unit that is on the verge of doing great things in the next month, so what do you think they would be telling their players down in the Richmond locker room right now when they gather to go over Xavier personnel? I think I can guess, it probably goes something like this; Terrell Holloway, really good with the ball. Gets in the lane, defends his butt off. He is really starting to shoot the ball well right now, we cannot disrespect him.

"What about Jordan Crawford, hey Kevin Anderson, you or Crawford are the best player in the conference, I guess we'll find out today who really is. Takes big shots, he can go to the basket, defends well. Big challenge on our hands today Richmond.

"Dante Jackson. When we were at home a few years ago during the NCAA Tournament watching on TV, Jackson was making big threes as a freshman against Georgia. Then he followed that up a few nights later versus West Virginia. I'm telling you this dude makes big shots in big games. Fellas this is a big game, we've never been in a game like this before.

"Jamel McLean, towards the beginning of the year he was inconsistent; sometimes here sometimes not. Right now he is the strongest rebounder in the conference. When a shot goes up there can be two or three defenders and he'll still get to the ball, go back up strong for a dunk, then talk smack to the referees on the way back down the floor. He's a nasty player.

"Jason Love, we didn't even recruit him. Don't underestimate him, he may play a little below the rim, but he is leading the conference in offensive rebounding percentage. He catches on the block, and if you are left unaware against him you're done. Doesn't matter, right hand or left hand, he'll kill you.

"Dudes off the bench like Mark Lyons; he might be the best defender in the conference. Kenny Frease, no other team in the league has size like that coming off the bench. Fellas we got our hands full."

Mack concluded, "That is what I believe they would be telling their team right now. I could go on and on, down the line. Fellas, today is your day, not Richmond's."

The first half was a back-and-forth tug of war that saw Xavier push out to the game's largest lead at seven. That was short lived however when Richmond's David Gonzalvez came back down the floor and hit a three-pointer to cut the lead to four points. Both Crawford for Xavier and Kevin Anderson for Richmond played tight in the first half in their head-to-head battle for the league's best player. Instead, it was Gonzalvez from Richmond and Terrell Holloway for Xavier who were the team's leading scorers at the half.

Mack spoke during his trip to the locker room, "I like the fact that we never sent them to the line that half, but we need to work on a few other things defensively right now. Richmond has us on our heels a bit with some middle ball screens they are running. We'll make that adjustment though. Richmond is going with a smaller lineup, we dominated inside, need to do more of that in the second half."

Mack retreated with his staff into their own personal locker room. The group will always meet by themselves before going across the hall to address the team during the latter part of halftime. When the coaches gathered Pat Kelsey was the first to speak, "We need to drive to the box or post it more; I really feel that is where we have the biggest advantage right now."

Mack said while looking over the stat sheet, "You know we had a couple of charge calls go against us when guys were standing right under the basket. That's bull, thanks for the rule change."

Mack had been referring to a recent rule change that stated a player could not take a charge when standing directly under the basket. Xavier had a couple of calls that they felt went against them in this area during the half when driving to the basket. Even though that was the case the staff felt that they had an advantage down on the low post, and would continue to drive with the ball in the second half.

When Mack addressed the team a few minutes later he wanted to stress one point each on both offense and defense, "Fellas, on defense we have to do away with what I call, 'Look-at-ya threes'. That happens when someone like Gonzalvez gets the balls and sort of starts bobbing and weaving with the ball. At that point there is no 'Princeton' sort of movement going on. He is simply in open-gym mode and looking to shoot. You need to recognize this and get a hand over his shooting pocket, make it hard for him to get into shooting position. We need to do a better job of that this half, understand?

"On offense; I have listened to people talk all year about how great Richmond is on defense by holding teams to 60 points a game. Well, we're at 38 right now, and if we get more movement in the half court I'm telling you we can score 80 points on them.

"Cheeks, when you have the ball don't hold it, because when you do five guys are defending on your dribble, get the ball out of your hands and move. Movement, driving with the ball and passing is where we can be more effective. Jamel, early in the game you drove, threw a bounce pass to Jason, easy two points. Fellas if we move on offense, and work the ball down low we'll win."

Much like the first half, the game went back and forth during the second half until Xavier pushed out to a five-point lead with two minutes to go before Richmond cut it to one after scoring on two straight possessions. Xavier's Jason Love had a chance to put the game away after making a put back on Dante Jackson's missed shot. Love was fouled, but missed the free throw that would have put Xavier up by four."

Instead, Richmond got the rebound, and out of a timeout got the ball into the hands of Gonzalvez, who made a three to tie the game with 26 seconds left on the clock. Mack quickly called a thirty second timeout and set up a play for Jordan Crawford. As the clock wound down to zero, the play didn't really space out the way Xavier envisioned, and Crawford drove right, did not get off a good shot, and missed.

Overtime.

Some of the fans in the stands were displaying the fact that they didn't understand why the play was for Crawford and not for a player like Holloway who was arguably having the better game. Mack's feeling on the situation was this, "Crawford is our best player on the floor; he has the best chance at working his way open for the last shot, with or without the ball. Plus, he has been in that position more than any other player on our team at various times throughout the season. I feel confident in all of my guys, but Jordan is the toughest matchup."

There were three ties and three lead changes in the first overtime period, and Love's tip-in at 1:41 evened the two squads at 70 apiece. Xavier again put together a last possession play with Crawford taking the final shot which didn't go down. Five more minutes of play.

In the second overtime, Xavier finally got things to fall their way. Led by Terrell Holloway, who scored Xavier's first seven points in the period, Xavier never trailed. Jason Love was sent to the line after Richmond had cut the lead to one and converted the first of his two free throws. Richmond rebounded the miss on the second, called timeout, and then ran the clock down to near zero when they got the ball inside to Justin Haroer; who missed the layup giving Xavier the win 78-76.

Mack was proud of the effort his team put forth when he spoke to them afterward, "Fellas in my opinion, the tougher team won today. We still won despite 20 turnovers and only 7 assists. I thought our effort level in the overtime was tremendous. The defensive effort that you guys put on Kevin Anderson, I know he ended up with 18 points, but for a long time I didn't even know he was out there. Great job, that's a really good team down the hall. You should be proud of yourselves.

"We have not gotten to the mountaintop, it's in sight, but we have not gotten there. Now we are down to 80 minutes to win a championship, one on the road and one at home. Tomorrow I want you to come in, practice hard, and be excited to be part of this team because we are about to do something special."

Xavier was special indeed over their last two regular season games. The first was a win at Fordham 82-56 before closing out the season with a convincing 93-72 win over St. Bonaventure in front of the home crowd at Cintas Center. The last home game was also an opportunity for the program and the fans to say goodbye to Jason Love. It was going to be his last home game in a Xavier uniform, and as expected it was an emotional night. After the win, which secured the fourth straight regular season A-10 crown, the team cut down the nets while letting their fans onto the court to celebrate. Mack addressed the crowd telling them that they would need their support in the coming weeks at both the A-10 Conference Championship and the NCAA Tournament.

It was high times at the Cintas Center, there were smiles all around the arena which carried over to the locker room after the game. Mack asked Jason Love to address the team which he did briefly, then Mack spoke, "You know I look around this room and one word comes to mind, change. Before the season started there was a lot of talk about how much change happened in our program. Many said it was one of the most tumultuous off seasons in recent memory for us with Derrick Brown leaving and me taking over for Coach Miller. Well sitting here tonight it doesn't look like much has changed to me. You guys are here with pieces of the net behind your ears, and are regular season champion of the A-10 for the fourth straight year in a row. You believed in the coaching staff and you worked your tails off all year, you should be proud of what you accomplished so far.

"With that being said here is my message moving forward, it's simple, it's twofold; enjoy tonight. I want you to take some pride in what you have done."

With that Mack turned around and wrote the name DeWaun Rose on the board. "His senior year Xavier had a team that went undefeated in the regular season, and then lost in the MCC conference championship in the first round to Wright State. DeWaun was a teammate of mine, and when we got back to town he and some of the other players went to a bar near the University of Cincinnati campus. They were excited, Selection Sunday was a few days away and there was no doubt that they were going to play. Xavier was picked to be a #6 or #7 seed. Well, some people started talking smack to DeWaun, and he finally got into it with someone. Eventually he was arrested, and because of that, he was suspended, and did not get to play in the NCAA.

"Now fellas, believe me, I'm not naïve, I've been in college, but understand, I don't want you to be that guy that makes a wrong decision. I don't want to get that call in the middle of the night telling me one of you is in jail. Nobody cares whether or not it's your fault, and that it was some other guy that was causing all of the trouble. Remember, that 'other guy' doesn't have a name, you do. Be smart when you are out with your friends or family this weekend.

"Now on to my second point; the A-10 tournament. It looks like we will be playing the winner of George Washington and either Dayton or Charlotte. It will probably be Charlotte, but if St. Louis wins later today at Dayton we will be looking at either Dayton or GW. Our game will be on Friday, so we'll leave here on Wednesday.

"Please, please, please don't believe people that tell you the conference tournament does not matter. I've won one three times as a coach and a player, and believe me, there is nothing like it. If we can go in there, and do a phenomenal job, it will make a huge difference in our NCAA seeding. I am having Mario Mercurio put together a spreadsheet that will show you how important it is to be a 4/5 seed vs. a 6/7 seed. If we go to Atlantic City and perform it can really help us. We have to be a team that goes there for a bigger reason than just winning the conference tournament, and that's gonna start on Monday when we get back."

Cheers went up all around the room as the players reveled not just in what they had accomplished to that point in the season, but they were also showing some of the emotion they had about looking forward to the next few weeks. In college basketball, for the average fan, it's all about March. A time when teams enter into their own conference championships, to either secure a higher seeding, or to hopefully make a run and win to gain an automatic entry into the NCAA tournament the following week. Conference tournament week is filled with all sorts of highlights, upsets, and last second shots; a hoop junkie's dream, but that is just the beginning.

The anticipation that every fan, player, and coach feels while waiting around on Selection Sunday to see where they may be headed to play next has become one of the more popular days on the sporting calendar. This was a fun time, this is what all of the hard practices, tough losses, and triumphant wins led up to.

Mack was well aware of the importance of the month ahead, "Programs are remembered most for the games they win in March, and we're no different. I think the experience gained throughout the year will only help. Every game is a road game, on a neutral floor against a really good team. We relish the challenge to see how good we can be."

Chapter 9

Post Season

As the Dayton Flyers and Xavier Musketeers dodged raindrops on their way to Boardwalk Hall in Atlantic City for their second round matchup in the Atlantic 10 Conference Championship, they were two teams heading into the same arena, yet going in vastly different directions. The 25-point loss suffered by Xavier on Dayton's home court had propelled the Musketeers on a seven game winning streak, eventually breaking into the Top 25 by the end of the regular season. Xavier had won a share of the A-10 regular season title, and was thought by many to be the favorite to win the conference title while in New Jersey. Xavier looked as though they were comfortably in the NCAA tournament. At the worst as a #6 seed, and at best, who knew how far up the seeding chart the team could vault with a decent showing over the weekend.

Dayton, meanwhile, struggled down the stretch. Ever since that mid-February matchup against Xavier, Dayton had gone 5-5 over their remaining schedule to limp into the A-10 Championship. The Flyers, more than likely, would need to beat Xavier, at the very least, to gain entry into the NCAA. Dayton suffered from the fact that they didn't have enough quality wins to offset their mounting losses, almost making it a certainty they would not receive an automatic bid.

Lastly, to further cement Dayton's fate, it appeared that no matter what happened in the A-10 Tournament, the league was probably only sending three teams to the NCAA; Temple, Richmond, and Xavier. It was widely recognized that a league like the A-10 would not get four teams into the NCAA, unless a lower seeded team won the conference championship.

Xavier players seemed to have a bit of a chip on their shoulder coming into the game. Dante Jackson had made some comments the prior day pointing to the fact that many of the Xavier players were a bit offended that the conference player of the year award went to Richmond's Kevin Anderson. Many inside the Xavier locker room felt that accolade should have gone to Jordan Crawford.

"We're not a team that needs a lot of outside influences to get us ready to play, but we felt like if the players took issue with some things on their own, that was ok too," said Mack prior to tipoff. There was no doubt that in player's language this was a "message" game.

Xavier began to deliver that message on their first possession when Jason Love threw down a thunderous dunk. It was a nice start that enabled Xavier to grab an early lead. But as the half wore on things were not clicking on offense, which enabled Dayton to climb ahead and push the lead out to as many as nine points. Xavier would fight back behind Jason Love's 11 first half points to cut the lead to five at the half.

Things, though, had gotten worse when the second half got underway. At the 11:16 mark Dayton's Josh Benson hit a three pointer to put the Flyers ahead by fifteen. It appeared as though the game was starting to slip away from Xavier when a funny thing happened; Dayton stopped scoring. Dayton would not hit another shot from the field until the 1:11 mark. By that point Xavier had been able to claw all the way back, and had even built a three point lead.

With under a minute to play Rob Lowcry of Dayton didn't help matters when he took a swing at Xavier's Terrell Holloway as Holloway began to reach in for a steal just as Lowery was attempting to call a time-out. A technical was called, and Holloway made both free throws giving Xavier a four point lead, which they would not relinquish, and went on to win the game 78-73. After pushing the lead to fifteen at 11:16 to go in the game, Xavier outscored Dayton 34-14 the rest of the way.

After completing the win against Dayton, Xavier knew they would be facing Richmond in the semifinals on Saturday. Xavier had now gone to the semifinals for the fifth straight year, and 11 of 15 years that they had been in the conference.

Dayton's short stay in the conference championship more than likely meant a bid to the National Invitation Tournament, also known as the NIT. It was going to be their only chance to continue postseason play. Mack spoke about Xavier's tenacity on the bus back to the hotel, "That game was defined by the word momentum. Dayton played very well for the first 30 minutes and we were in a tough spot. But I was pleased with how our kids responded, never giving in to the large deficit we were facing. This team is resilient."

When Xavier and Richmond hooked up in their semifinal matchup the next day the game looked very similar to the one the two teams played a few weeks prior. The game was a back-and-forth battle the whole way; after Richmond's David Gonzalvez tied the game on a three point play, Xavier came back and scored on their next three possessions to push the lead to six. Before the end of the half, Gonzalvez made a pair of free throws to cut the lead down to four in favor of Xavier, 37-33.

Three straight turnovers by Richmond early into the second half enabled Xavier to push the lead to nine. Xavier was on the brink of putting the game away when they suddenly stumbled through a four and a half minute stretch in which they only scored one field goal. During that stretch Richmond capitalized, seizing the lead by one. The lead, however, was short lived; Xavier finally woke up on offense when Terrell Holloway hit a three-pointer to put the Musketeers back on top by two.

At the 3:00 mark Xavier moved out in front by five when Kenny Frease made a jumper in the paint. Again, Xavier had the chance to salt things away but frittered away chances on their next two possessions allowing Richmond's David Gonzalvez to get loose again and score on another three-pointer cutting the lead to two. Richmond called timeout, which allowed Mack to set up a play for Crawford. That play worked when Crawford scored in the lane to get the lead back to four. But, less than ten seconds later Richmond's Kevin Anderson scored from the field cutting the lead in half back down to two with 46 seconds left.

On Xavier's next possession, when Terrell Holloway missed a running layup, Richmond got the ball. Xavier's Dante Jackson quickly reached in and stole the ball before he was fouled; that sent Jackson to the line with a chance to put the game away with two made free throws. Richmond called timeout wanting to give Jackson some time to think about the upcoming shots.

Jackson returned to the line after the timeout and looked calm and confident before shooting the first free throw. Jackson sent the ball on the way, and missed. Richmond's Gonzalvez got the rebound, fired the ball to Kevin Anderson streaking down the court, where he drove through the lane and made the game tying shot with seconds to spare, sending the game to overtime.

In the Xavier huddle there was no talk about what just happened, just instructions from Mack about what the team needed to do to win the game in overtime, "Those times are tough, you are trying to digest what just happened, but you can't let the players dwell on it. We try and look at it like we have five minutes to go in the game, and we still have a good chance to win."

Richmond's David Gonzalvez set the tone quickly, hitting a three point shot to open the overtime. Richmond grabbed a lead they would never relinquish over the next five minutes. Richmond had defeated Xavier and now looked forward to playing Temple in the conference championship the next day.

Watching other conference games later that evening Mack spoke about the game with Richmond earlier in the evening, and what lie ahead, "Two very talented, equally well prepared teams. Neither team wanted to lose. A couple of free throws and we're playing in the finals. But, it wasn't to be and we move on. Kevin Anderson and David Gonzalvez showed why they're all-league performers. I'm disappointed, and will be tonight, but starting tomorrow we think NCAA Tournament."

The team departed Atlantic City the next morning and was back in Cincinnati by early afternoon. The team decided that they would meet at Longneck's, the sports bar near Mack's house, for the selection show later that evening. The team arrived by bus around 5:00 and over the next hour had a nice dinner while watching some of the weekend's highlights on the big screen. By 6:00 the place was packed with Xavier fans in anticipation to see who the team would play.

Mack and his staff seemed relatively loose as the show began, looking like any other patrons sitting at a table watching as the first teams were announced on CBS. Mack said there was not much that had been done as far as trying to figure out who Xavier might play, "All we really try and do leading up to the NCAA is keep an eye on things and get a sense of where we may be seeded and who potential opponents might be. You may keep an eye on teams you feel may be on that list. You build a film library throughout the year to be prepared, but it's far from an exact science. It's more of a waiting game than anything."

Mack's had his own take on where and when the team might play before the selection show started, "Doesn't matter to us where and when we play. No matter where we go we tell our kids this is a four-team, two-game tournament, win your first game and the second one two days later, then we get to go to another four team tournament the following weekend. If you can do that for three weeks in a row, you'll win it all.

"It's all in an effort to maintain focus at this time of year. It's much like we do when we talk about shrinking down a game into four minute wars. During the NCAA we try and take the approach that you are in a four team bracket instead of looking at the thing as a whole. This way it becomes a little more manageable to comprehend and maintain focus."

There was not much surprise when CBS showed the first four #1 seeds with Kansas in the Midwest, Syracuse in the West, Kentucky in the East, and Duke in the South. Those four teams had been near the top of the rankings most of the year. Three of the four, Kentucky, Duke, and Kansas were also coming off having won their respective conference championships. CBS first went through the Midwest bracket detailing the road that Kansas may have to take to Indianapolis before going to break.

Mack and his staff continued to wait patiently as CBS returned from the break. Knowing that you are in the tournament is completely different than sitting on the bubble, as Mack's Evansville Aces were during his freshman year, "We made it in the West region as an at-large #11 seed, meaning we were one of the last teams in. The hardest part was that CBS didn't show our bracket until after a couple of commercials. We were ecstatic when we saw our name, but man, that wait, especially until later in the show, is no fun at all. When you are pretty confident you are in, it makes it much easier to watch."

CBS moved down to the West bracket which had Syracuse as the #1 seed. Many NCAA forecasters were projecting that Xavier would be in that bracket as a #6 or #7 seed. The matchups were coming on to the screen one game at a time, and after the Vanderbilt vs. Murray State game in San Jose one could see that the #6 vs. #11 matchup in Milwaukee would be announced next. Mack leaned over to his staff and quietly said to them, "I have a good feeling that this is going to be us." The 6/11 game flashed up, and it was.

A cheer went up throughout the bar when it was shown that Xavier was indeed the #6 seed and would be facing the #11 seed Minnesota on Friday. While many people were cheering and high fiving each other Mack intently continued to watch the screen to see who Xavier would have to face in the next round. The answer came quickly when the next game was shown; #3 Pittsburgh or #14 seed Oakland.

Mack let out big sigh after all of the teams were announced, "It certainly won't be easy. It will be interesting to see what happens down the line if we make it to Salt Lake City for the regionals. Two teams that beat us, Butler and Kansas State, are also in our bracket. I think it speaks to the quality of our schedule that six of the seven teams that beat us, with the exception of Dayton, have made it in."

So, there it was. After a season that was filled with all sorts of twists and turns, up and downs, doubt and belief, it was official. Chris Mack had been able to guide the Xavier Musketeers back to the NCAA Tournament. It was Xavier's fifth consecutive appearance. Mack continued a streak at Xavier that had now seen the last six coaches, going back to Bob Staak in 1983, gain entry into the NCAA.

Mack was also one of only two coaches in the tournament leading their teams during the first year on the job, the other was John Calipari at Kentucky. That meant Mack was the only rookie head coach in the entire tournament. Not a bad start to the coaching career.

There was not much time to reflect on that though, Mack was already considering the challenges that lay ahead having to play Minnesota. The Gophers were led by Tubby Smith, who was in his third season after coming over from Kentucky where he had won a national championship in 1998.

Soon after the show concluded the team and staff began to file out of the restaurant to get on the bus and head back over to the Cintas Center. Mack said that he wanted to get the team together briefly before he and his staff began preparing for Minnesota. When Mack got the team settled down into their locker room back at the arena the message was succinct, "Guys tonight we learned that we are going to participate in the Milwaukee Invitational this weekend. Joining us is your opponent Minnesota. Pittsburgh will play Oakland in the other game; we'll play the winner on Sunday. Our goal is simple - to go up there and win both games.

"Many of you have been here before, some haven't, but I want to remind everyone to be respectful of Minnesota and stay away from making any sort of predictions for the game. That's a distraction we do not need at this point. We'll start breaking down some film to have personnel for you, then we'll have two days of light practice before leaving on Wednesday."

Mack ended the meeting and headed upstairs with his staff for what would be a very long evening, "We don't know very much about Minnesota. They just made it to the finals of the Big Ten championship, so they are certainly a hot team. With Tubby Smith as their coach, it goes without saying that they are well schooled, and will be prepared for us Friday. Tonight will be a late one, but this is what we live for."

Monday morning, after hours of film review, Mack took a short break, heading home for a quick bite to eat and a shower, then, back over to the office for endless media requests during the remainder of the day.

In that short amount of time Mack sounded as though he had been scouting Minnesota all year long, "They have an incredible shooter in Blake Hoffarber who is shooting over 40% from beyond the three point line. Devoe Joseph is solid at the point. He really does a nice job of handling the ball for them."

One of Mack's initial concerns was going to be matching up against Minnesota's size, "Their frontcourt is bigger than ours, Colton Iverson and Ralph Sampson will make rebounding a challenge. Our post players are going to need to finish strong when Minnesota has a lot of size in the game."

Mack already had formed an initial game plan as he made his way back across the Ohio River on the I-471 bridge, "On defense we need to be aware that their post players are not real efficient when shooting the ball, so we need to be ready to rebound those misses and not give them multiple shots on each possession, and I feel we can defend that pretty well. A lot of their scoring comes from the perimeter where they shoot the ball pretty well, so it will be important for guys like Terrell, Cheeks, Jordan, and Dante to be aggressive and pressure the ball."

On offense the emphasis was going to be on ball movement, "We want to move the ball in the half court to try and get their big men out of the paint to defend us. We also want to try and get some scoring in transition, again to take advantage of the big men moving slowly on the court. Minnesota likes to get teams into a half-court offense; they defend that setup better than a team getting up and down the floor; which is one of our strengths."

Wednesday came quickly, and when the team arrived in Milwaukee they appeared loose and ready to play. Mack had commented that they were on a pretty even keel, not too wide-eyed at the whole event, and seemingly ready to play. "At the beginning of the tourney we don't want guys thinking ahead to the Final Four, we don't want them to get caught up in where the results will take us. Let's just keep things to a minimum and not look beyond the next possession."

Thursday was a light day with an open practice at the Bradley Center and a press conference to follow. Mack said that being on the NCAA stage in the past is a big advantage, "During the NCAA things are a lot more regimented as far as your schedule, and there are bigger crowds of fans and media than during the regular season. For teams that have not gone through that before it can be pretty overwhelming. We have, so it's just another day at the office for us."

Even though Mack had been to the tournament before as both a coach and player, this year was still a first of sorts being that he was the head coach. Mack was asked to comment when he met with the media on what it was like this time around since he was now 'the man', "I don't know if I'm 'the man'. I get off the bus and I've got my four-year-old and three-year-old and they're screaming at me to get their camera and stuff like that. So I wouldn't say I'm 'the man'. To me, and maybe it should be more of a story line, but I just feel like it's business as usual.

"I've been in the NCAA tournament a lot as a player, as director of operations, as an assistant coach. And other than me standing a whole lot more during the course of the game, I just feel like Xavier's used to being in the NCAA tournament. And we're excited like we always are, and we'll be ready to go on Friday. Don't make anything bigger of it than that. I think good players make good coaches. Roy Williams is a really good coach. He's not playing in this tournament. The same with Ben Howland. I'm blessed to have really good kids, kids I enjoy coaching that have done a really good job, improving as the season's gone along."

When Friday's coverage began on CBS, the Xavier game was the first to tip off, so for a short while the whole country would get a chance to watch the Xavier/Minnesota matchup before being switched to other regional games starting a short time later. As the game unfolded one of Mack's concerns started coming to fruition, Xavier's ability to score in the low post, "We were able to get the ball inside like we wanted to at times, but it seemed like every shot we took was blocked by Iverson or Sampson."

When Xavier had the opportunity to get off an open shot they were not converting. Xavier only scored 26 points at the half, but had been able to keep the game tied by virtue of good defensive pressure on Minnesota. Mack and his staff felt upbeat to be tied despite not playing real well overall. "Actually I had to calm the staff down on their excitement over the fact that we had 15 offensive rebounds because there was a reason for that; most of those are all the blocked shots we're getting back in our face. That stat doesn't mean a whole lot," Mack said during halftime.

"We had to get better shots, and we weren't going to get them around the rim. We were doubled and tripled every time. We were going to have to kick out, and a lot of this depended on the ability of our big men to move the ball when needed." Mack made that exact point to his post players in the locker room, "Fellas you need to recognize if you have the ball and find yourself in a one-on-one in situation, and you're getting a shot blocked, that's one thing. But when it's one versus two, you have to be quick to see that and realize, 'hey two on me, someone is open'. Somebody has to be open on the perimeter. Quick ball movement will beat these guys."

Mack then addressed the rest of the team, "Listen fellas, for us to play as poorly as we did and be right there against a good team means we're fine. Let's just come out more composed in the second half, do a better job on the glass, and get the win."

Xavier fell behind by one at the 18:32 mark of the second half, but behind improved play from the big men, Xavier started to build a lead. "Kenny and Jason did a much better job in the second half. After 10 blocks in the first half, Minnesota only had one in the second.

"Later in the game our guards started to get into the lane a bit more and disrupt Minnesota's defense which opened up a lot of good looks for us."

Xavier pushed the lead to double digits at the 5:36 mark on a jumper by Terrell Holloway, but then had to rely on defense to maintain that lead when they failed to score over the next three and a half minutes. Xavier came up big on defense during that stretch, holding Minnesota to just four points.

A three point basket by Jordan Crawford with 38 seconds left ultimately provided the final nail in the coffin for Minnesota. The lead now stood at nine points, which Xavier pushed to 11 by the final buzzer, and won 65-54.

Mack was asked for his overall feelings shortly after the game, "Well, we had a lot of respect coming into this game for Minnesota. They did an unbelievable job down the stretch to regroup. They dealt with a lot of adversity during the season, were able to pull together at the right time of the year and go into this game ready to go. And I thought in the first half our kids - we struggled finishing around the basket. We got into areas we wanted to get with the basketball, but we weren't able to finish around the rim. And you have to credit Minnesota's size and athleticism around the basket."

Mack said that the ability to make adjustments they needed to at the half was the deciding factor. One case in point that Mack pointed out afterwards was driving the ball into the lane to pick up defenders, then quickly kicking the ball out to someone who was open,

"You know Colton Iverson and Damian Johnson were doing an unbelievable job of blocking shots on the weak side during the first half. We had to get the ball into the lane to get their attention, then kick it out. We made that point continually to the kids, but sometimes you have to learn the hard way."

Lastly, Mack revealed a bit of a secret that he had held back from his players, "I kept reminding myself, although I didn't tell our kids, I don't think Minnesota had ever recovered from a deficit of seven points or more during the season, so, once we got it up there, I was hoping that would hold true, and it did."

One story that had not gotten out to the press before the start of the game was Xavier's reaction to an article that Jim Souhan had written in the Star Tribune. The gist of the article was that Minnesota should hardly be considered the underdog for a variety of reasons; Mack was a rookie coach who would be in over his head versus a veteran winner like Tubby Smith.

Xavier's higher seeding would prove to be irrelevant because of the home-court advantage Minnesota would enjoy playing in close-by Milwaukee. Minnesota played in a power conference, the Big10, and Xavier came from the Atlantic10. Souhan felt that the Big10 was full of teams that should be in the tournament every year and the Atlantic 10 was made up of teams that had to overachieve just to get into the tournament. Souhan was of the opinion that having to face the rigors of a schedule such as the Big10 would favor Minnesota.

The article was in the Friday morning edition, so having hit the streets after the Thursday news conference nobody had a chance to ask Mack his thoughts. During the post-game press conference it was finally addressed by Mack publicly when asked how he thought Xavier's talent level compared to Minnesota coming into the game, "Well, I worried about their size. I also worried in the fact that they had three kids on the perimeter that shoot the eyes out of the ball. But there's different ways to motivate kids. And we're tired of being the little engine that could. We're a really good program. And our kids aren't scared to play anybody. We don't always win, but we're not afraid to compete. And…Jim Souhan, from the Star Tribune, thanks for the motivation to tell our kids that we should be fodder against Minnesota.

"Our kids are used to this stage. We've played a lot of NCAA tournament games. We've been very successful. It's my charge and our kids' charge to continue to do that." Mack said the article did bother him and the rest of the team, "Yeah, it sort of rubbed us the wrong way. We're not afraid to compare our record to anyone else in the country over the past few years. We may not have any National Championship banners to hang in Cintas Center, yet, but our regular season record and post season performance is better than most, that's a fact."

Mack left the press conference to meet up with the rest of his staff who was already out near the court watching the Pittsburgh/Oakland matchup. Xavier was going to face the winner on Sunday. During the game associate head coach Pat Kelsey kept his eye on Oakland, while assistant coach Travis Steele monitored the actions of Pittsburgh. Despite what many people think, a decent amount of scouting went into these two teams even before Xavier beat Minnesota.

Pittsburgh dominated throughout and won easily 89-66. Xavier was now going to face the team that ousted them from the tournament during last year's Sweet 16 matchup, which ended up being Sean Miller's last game. When the game was complete, the coaches made their way back to the hotel to continue their preparation for Pittsburgh. Later that evening the staff presented the scouting report to the team.

Mack's wife Christi commented on the how different things are come tournament time because of the compressed schedule, "Usually the girls and I would stay with Chris, but when we got to the NCAA tournament we stayed in separate rooms. I barely spoke to Chris while we were in Milwaukee. It was nonstop preparation for Pittsburgh once the Minnesota game ended. You don't have the luxury of having a couple of days to prepare for your next opponent, and because of that we rarely spoke."

Once the players had filed back up to their rooms for the night Mack gave his initial assessment of Pittsburgh, "Well, whether it's the offensive end or defensive end, Pitt is a very challenging team. On offense, I think they're more perimeter-oriented than they are post-oriented. They do a good job sharing the ball, so we're going to have to make sure that everybody on the defensive end is locked in and understands their assignment."

One of the main points that Mack and his staff had stressed to the team minutes earlier was the fact that Xavier had to be the tougher team, "Pitt was going to make you work for everything; when a shot goes up, all of their players crash the boards, you don't see that too often, everyone has to be on their toes.

"We told the guys that even though they were tired tonight, they had to find a way to be ready come Sunday. They had to be prepared for the fact that they were going to get fouled, have to fight through hard screens, and that they couldn't be the type of player looking to the referee for help. They were going to have to deal with it on their own.

"During the year Pitt had prided themselves on being able to win the tough games, and they did, no question. But you know what, and we wanted to get this into the team's head, that we were just as tough. We have every right to be thought of as a tough team like Pitt."

Mack highlighted what he felt were the priorities on both ends of the floor, "On defense we recognize that Ashton Gibbs is their best player by far. He does it all; range from beyond three point line, lot of shot fakes, good at moving the ball. It will be key to pressure him. On the inside, if we can limit them to one shot, don't let them get second chance points, we can win. Pittsburgh also has a tendency to go long stretches without scoring, which should only help us.

"On offense we need to move the ball. We believe that one-on-ones are going to be tough, so we need our guys to move the ball, similar to the second half of the Minnesota game. We need to play with a lot of pace. If we do that we think that their center, Gary McGhee will have a hard time keeping up. Lastly, if we can set some ball screens in transition, I think Pitt will have a tough time defending those."

Time moves quickly during the NCAA Tournament, when Mack, his staff, and the rest of the team filed back into the Bradley Center it had been roughly 48 hours since their win on Friday. The Xavier/Pittsburgh game was a late tipoff, near 5:00 pm in the east. That meant Xavier would probably get some more national exposure since most of the coverage would switch over when other games concluded.

There had been some talk that this was a revenge game for Xavier since they were facing a team that had knocked them out of last year's tournament. Mack didn't really see it that way, "Even though the same names are on the front of the uniform a lot has changed for both programs. I think the revenge idea is more for the fans than anything."

Mack liked what he saw from his players as the game got underway, "I really liked what we were doing on defense. We just defended the ball really well, played tough and aggressive, and were able to use that to build a decent lead."

Ashton Gibbs from Pittsburgh made a jumper with 9:17 left in the half to put the Panthers up by three. Then Pittsburgh entered into one of their dead zones not scoring again until 3:26 left in the half. Xavier's defense had a lot to do with that dry spell, "Their guys on the perimeter were not getting good looks, and we really limited them to one shot. At that point we felt like we saw Pitt starting to question themselves," said Mack.

Xavier's confidence grew from that, and they were able to build a 13-point lead before the Panthers were able to put any more points on the board. Dante Jackson continued to turn his game up a notch when it came to the NCAA, burying two big three pointers during that stretch, "Dante's fearless in March. He's shown that in that past, and the Pitt game was no exception. Dante just seemed to infuse the rest of the group."

To Pittsburgh's credit they were able to keep Xavier in their sights during the closing minutes of the first half. Pittsburgh showed a little more defensive pressure that held Xavier to only two points in the last three minutes, and started to get things going more on the offensive side of the ball.

"We said a big part of stopping their offense was to not let them get multiple shots on possession, which they did near the end of the half. That got them back into the game, basically cutting the lead in half, and only being down seven," Mack said of Pittsburgh's comeback.

Mack spoke about the halftime, "While we were disappointed to have let them back in the game, overall I liked a lot of what I was seeing. Pittsburgh was as physical as we anticipated, but our kids were able to match them in that area. That was huge. I think Pitt knew they had a tough team on their hands that was not going to back down from them in the second half.

"We just told the team to stand their ground the first four minutes of the next half. Pitt will try and go to their usual card and try and bully their way back into the game, if they could withstand that out of the gate, they'd be fine."

Before heading back out for the second half Mack said that he tried to get an assessment of each of his players to see where they stood, "I liked what I saw. Instead of seeing a group that was rattled by the lead they had given up, I saw a team that knew what they needed to do in order to win, and felt confident they were going to get the job done."

When the bell rang for the second half, it was Xavier playing the role of bully. Jason Love muscled his way for a rebound off a Nasir Robinson missed layup and got the ball up the floor to Xavier's yearlong go-to man, Jordan Crawford, who buried a three-pointer to move the lead back up to ten. A short time later Pittsburgh's Brad Wanamaker put back an Ashton Gibbs miss, and was fouled. That sent each team to the bench for the under 16-minute timeout. Even though Pittsburgh had won the first four-minute war 6-5, Xavier had been able to stand their ground as the coaches instructed.

Wanamaker made the free throw out of the timeout to complete the three-point play and Xavier's lead was down to five. "I really thought the next two possessions spoke about the heart of our team. We get down the floor on offense and Terrell gets the ball into Love for an emphatic dunk, then we hold them to one shot on defense, get the rebound, and Jordan hits a three in transition. Boom, just like that, we are back up ten," commented Mack on the team's explosiveness on offense.

Xavier wasn't done; the defense grabbed another rebound off of an Ashton Gibbs miss and Crawford scored two more to push the lead to 12. That led Pittsburgh to call a timeout and regroup. The break in play worked for the Panthers, scoring on their next three possessions, cutting the lead back to six at the next TV timeout. Pittsburgh was in the midst of cutting the lead all the way back down to one, before Jason Love was fouled and made both free throws to open the lead back up to three with just under 8 minutes remaining.

Mack didn't like what he was seeing and called a timeout. During that timeout he made a decision that in the end may have been the deciding factor; he instructed his players to move to zone defense, "Pitt seemed to be on a roll offensively and we felt that if we threw a little zone at them it may make them think a bit and disrupt the flow of what they were doing."

It worked.

Xavier held Pitt to just four points over the next four minutes while building the lead to five, 61-56. A block by Jason Love on a Brad Wanamaker shot got a fast break going then ended in a Jordan Crawford dunk that pushed Xavier's lead to seven with just over two minutes to go. Crawford's dunk was Xavier's last field goal of the game.

Pitt's Gilbert Brown nailed a three in the next possession then fouled Crawford on the other end sending him to the line for two free throws. Crawford made both, so after that quick exchange, Pittsburgh had cut into the lead by one and trailed by six, 65-59.

When Terrell Holloway fouled Ashton Gibbs on Pittsburgh's next possession that put both teams in the double bonus, meaning Gibbs would be going to the line for two shots. Gibbs made the first, missed the second, and Jordan Crawford grabbed the rebound.

65-60.

Mack quickly called timeout, "I just wanted to make sure we were all on the same page, it was a big possession. We figured they were going to foul, and I wanted to make sure that we had the ball in Terrell's hands." At that point in the early evening, with a little less than a minute to go in the Xavier/Pittsburgh game, there were only seventeen teams left playing Division I college basketball. The rest of the second round games were complete, and the winner of this game would round out the Sweet Sixteen.

As Mack suspected, Pittsburgh did foul Holloway on Xavier's next trip down the floor. Holloway made both, giving Xavier a 67-60 lead with 35 seconds left on the clock. Pittsburgh screamed up the floor and got the ball to Gilbert Brown who drained a three cutting the lead to four. Pittsburgh's head coach Jamie Dixon quickly called timeout.

Mack huddled his players wanting to prepare them for Pittsburgh's next foul. The next sequence was eerily similar to the one that had preceded it; Crawford made both free throws to open the lead back to six points, then Pittsburgh hustled down the floor getting the ball into Brown's hands who again made another three pointer. The lead was now down to three, 69-66, with 15 seconds to go.

Mack again called for a timeout. This was getting repetitive. When the teams came out of the timeout, Pittsburgh fouled, Xavier made both free throws, then Pittsburgh came back down the floor and scored, but this time only two. The score was 71-68. When the ball was inbounded by Xavier, Pittsburgh fouled Dante Jackson stopping the clock with 5 seconds left. As Jackson stood at the line it was an eerily similar situation to what he faced a week earlier during the A-10 semifinal game against Richmond; a chance to ice the game away with two made free throws. If Jackson missed, the other team would have a chance to tie the game and send it into overtime.

Jackson missed both.

Mack said at that point, "The fact that the situation was nearly the same as the one Dante faced in the A-10, I don't really think about stuff like that at that point in a game. I am so focused on making sure the kids know what they need to do next, regardless of what happens. Unfortunately, it happened, so we dealt with it."

Pittsburgh grabbed the rebound and threw the ball down the floor to Ashton Gibbs who took a three-pointer that missed. Game over, Xavier wins!

Wait a minute, not quite so fast.

At that moment if you were a Xavier fan you may have considered throwing up because the officials were huddling to determine if there was any time left on the clock.

"I did sort of feel like I was back at Hinkle Fieldhouse there for a minute," Mack said as the officials agreed to put .3 seconds back on the clock. Pittsburgh would have one last desperation shot to tie the game, "We kept telling the players, off of the inbound make sure you are defending outside the three-point line. There was no reason to be inside of that line, there was no doubt Pitt was going to shoot a three. There was too little time on the clock, so a two-point basket was meaningless. Oh yeah, and one other thing, please don't foul."

Xavier didn't foul as Pittsburgh's Brad Wanamaker barely got off a three from the corner that missed. Finally it was over, Xavier was moving on. Mack spoke about his thoughts at the conclusion of the game, "During the handshake with the other team I just kept thinking how proud I was to lead this group of kids. They did everything we asked of them, they never backed down, and never quit, and because of that we were going to be one of only two programs in the last three years to have advanced to the Sweet 16; us and Michigan State. Not too shabby."

Mack spoke to an exhausted team afterward, "Fellas, I can't say enough about the effort you gave tonight, that was one hell of an effort. Let's enjoy this one because there is hardly a better feeling in college basketball than getting to move on to the second weekend. Let's enjoy it on our way back home, then start to get refocused because we have a quick turnaround for our game on Thursday.

"This weekend we were able to come up here and win the 'Milwaukee Invitational' and next weekend we are going to try and win the 'Salt Lake Invitational' starting against a team we are very familiar with in Kansas State. We learned a lot from our trip out there in December. Let's use that to our advantage, but for now enjoy today's win."

Mack's enthusiasm carried out into the hallway where he spoke about what he saw from his players so far in the NCAA, "We're starting to play better offensively and really share the ball. I know Jordan's getting a lot of attention. Very well deserved, but he's making some plays where he's passing, giving up the ball. Some of the plays I showed our guys after the Minnesota game offensively were as good as I've seen all year, sharing the ball, making the extra pass. When teams play like that on the offensive end and we stick to the defensive intensity I think this program's known for, we're going to be a tough out."

Even though Xavier played as solidly as anyone else the first weekend of the tournament they were not darlings of the national media heading into the regionals. Teams seeded much lower than Xavier seemed to be grabbing most of the headlines; Northern Iowa had knocked of Kansas, unheralded 12th seeded Cornell from the

Ivy League had beaten Wisconsin and would face #1 seeded Kentucky next, St. Mary's, a 10th seed, had gotten past #2 seeded Villanova punching their ticket into the next round.

The notion that Xavier was overachieving again in the NCAA showed in some of the questions that the players and Mack had to face when they met with the media after the Pittsburgh game. Jason Love responded a bit testily after having been asked what Xavier's identity was as a mid-major, "I don't feel like we're a mid-major at all. You look at our schedule; we played some of the best teams in the country. And I mean I don't know a lot of mid-majors that make three consecutive Sweet 16s. So you can throw that out of the door right now. And maybe media will start getting us a little more attention. We'll see."

Mack had to answer many of the same questions when he took the podium shortly after the players, "we don't look at ourselves as anything but being a high-major program, from the way we travel to the way we recruit to the amenities our kids enjoy. If you've ever been to our building on campus, it's one of the nicest on-campus arenas in the country. We've been doing some great things with our program for the last 25 years. We've had 14 NBA players since 1993. We've won multiple championships. Only us and Michigan State have been in the Sweet 16 the last three years. I think those things speak for themselves. I think sometimes other schools may get more publicity because we're in a hotbed area for college basketball. You could look 90 miles or 100 miles east, west, north, and south and you have some tremendous programs. From the Louisvilles to the UKs, the IUs, Ohio State. But you check our track record, it's pretty good."

Even though there were numerous questions surrounding the topic of how to label Xavier, Mack knew what sort of team he had in the locker room behind him before the team left the arena, "I don't care what people want to call us, at the end of the day I know what we have behind that door, a group of very, very competitive kids. When Pat Kelsey came on board, after leaving Wake Forest, the one thing he really talked about was he couldn't believe how competitive our kids were. And it's really shown itself throughout the entire year. When we took a couple of losses, we were able to regroup; we never lost consecutive games all year. And I think that says a lot about our kids and the makeup they have."

Mack summed up a long weekend with this final thought, "You know what, it's about the kids. That's what Coach Prosser used to say. We'd get a huge win and he would be sitting on the side watching our guys celebrate. I don't want to be the coach that runs out to half court and kisses the logo when we win. I'm just about our team. And you're a good coach when you have good players. Fortunately, we have some really competitive kids that want to continue on this tournament journey. I am honored to lead them along the way."

Chapter 10

How Sweet It Was

When the team returned to Cincinnati the city was euphoric over their win against Pittsburgh, and looking forward to exacting a little revenge on Kansas State in a few days.

"We wanted to make sure the players kept their focus when they got back home. I know it was a big deal that we had won two games, that's a great accomplishment, but we had a short schedule and needed to stay intent on Kansas State," Mack said during a light shoot around on Monday.

The players had been given updated personnel on Kansas State. Notes on each player had not changed much since the two teams' last meeting in December. There was still the double threat of Denis Clemente and Jacob Pullen in the backcourt which was arguably the best in the country. Down low Jason Love would have his hands full with Curtis Kelly and Jamar Samuels. Kansas State also had depth off the bench that head Coach Frank Martin was not afraid to use.

In Mack's mind though a lot had changed since the loss in December, "We are certainly a much better team than the first time we played. That was our first real road test of the season and we failed. But I thought it made our kids and our team a lot stronger and a lot better because of it. I think we've gotten better on both ends of the floor since that time. We certainly improved offensively. I think we've been a team that has had that inside-outside balance that you need. I think defensively we've continued to progress from day one. We didn't play necessarily a bad game defensively against Kansas State; we just had no answer for them on the backboard. That's something that causes a lot of opponents' problems with Kansas State.

"Since then though, these kids have shown a lot of heart, and sort of created their own identity; a team that plays with passion, and will never quit. I know they are looking forward to this challenge, not to get back at a team that beat them earlier, but a challenge in the sense that they know with each win they can write a new chapter in our program's history. Kansas State had a lot to do with the defeat we suffered in Manhattan, Kansas. They're a very physical team. It was our first true road test of the season. We certainly didn't pass it."

For Xavier the turnaround between the Pittsburgh game and the Kansas State game would be quick; the team arrived in Cincinnati late Sunday night after their second round win, and would be leaving in two short days for Salt Lake City.

Mario Mercurio had arranged for the team to have their own closed practice at a facility previously used by the Utah Jazz that would lead right into the obligatory open practice at Energy Solutions Arena on Wednesday with a press conference to follow.

Similar to the first meeting between Xavier and Kansas State in December, Mack still felt the two main areas of attention should be focused on rebounding and the defensive pressure that the Wildcats would bring. "KState denies the ball everywhere, not just in passing lanes, but all over the court. We didn't handle that as well as we should have the first time around and needed to make sure we were ready this time," Mack said when speaking about Xavier's preparation for the game, "I think the beauty of Kansas State's philosophy is they don't necessarily key in on one guy. They just make it tough on every player on the floor for your team. You generally don't get a lot of ball reversal because they pressure passing lanes.

"KState hasn't changed much since December; they play physical, have a really potent backcourt, and like to get it down low. We noticed that their big men don't handle the ball real well out from the lane, so we wanted to present a defense that would make entry passes down low hard to accomplish."

Lastly, Mack said on defense Xavier would need to keep Kansas State out of transition, "Pullen and Clemente are very good players, and we need do as good of a job as we can keeping those two out of transition which is easier said than done.

"When the shot goes up, that's where Kansas State is at their best. They're a terrific offensive rebounding team. They're more than just Pullen and Clémente. I think that's the key to the game."

As the team gathered in the locker room prior to tipoff, cheers could be heard raining down from the arena as Butler was putting the finishing touches on an upset win of #1 seed Syracuse. Butler had held the first two teams they played in the tournament to less than 60 points; Syracuse was no different, with Butler winning by the final score of 63-59. Many Xavier fans were now giddy at the thought of being able to get back at Butler for the "clock game" by beating the Bulldogs to go to the Final Four.

Of course, beating Kansas State was not a foregone conclusion as Mack said, "At the time the players really never gave it much thought. Looking ahead is the job of the assistants, the players kept their focus on the game in front of them, just as they had all year long."

Mack had given some extra thought to what he wanted to say to his players before the game. They had faced a lot of questions in Milwaukee the weekend prior about being a mid-major program, and what it felt like to be overachieving again at this time of year.

Mack looked to a book he had read within the last year titled *Born to Run* by Christopher McDougall. It was a story about a tribe in Mexico, the Tarahumara. The culture of this tribe is that for everything they do they run, sometimes running multiple marathons in a day.

Mack's point was that the tribe is able to perform this seemingly impossible feat because running is simply part of their culture, it's what they do because no one has put limitations in their minds. Mack made the analogy for the team, "They don't allow anyone to put them in a box and label or define who they should be. Don't let people do the same for you; define yourselves. You deserve to be here, you deserve to win, and I have every confidence in you that you'll do that tonight."

Mack spoke on his way to the floor as the team ran out in front of him, "I know these guys have a confidence in each other to get this done. If we can improve upon some of the things we did poorly in Manhattan earlier in the year we stand a good chance of moving on. Kansas State is not going to roll over no matter what the scoreboard says. Like Pittsburgh, they like to bully with their physicality sometimes, but we just proved last weekend that we can be the tougher team when playing against that style."

Things were a bit wild when the ball was finally tipped and the game began with each team missing shots on their first possessions down the floor. A minute and a half into a scoreless game Mack called for a lob play to Crawford who slammed the ball down for the first points, "That was a play we had put in for Jordan just before the start of the game. I thought the time was right to call for it and it worked. I felt it would soften their ball denial early."

Unfortunately it didn't.

When the teams both broke from their huddles after the first official timeout Kansas State held an 8-4 lead, but would soon open that lead to 19-4 over the next few minutes of play. Mack said of that spurt, "They were getting production from everyone, scored a couple of times on fast breaks, and pretty much rebounded everything in sight."

Dante Jackson finally got Xavier back on the board when he hit a three-point shot before the next media timeout near the 12-minute mark. Mack assessed his team's state of mind as they came to the sideline, "When we got the team in the huddle I actually liked what I saw; nobody was wide eyed and everyone seemed pretty calm. Dante's three was a huge lift. We said to the kids, 'listen we have been here before, remember the Dayton game in the A-10 a few weeks ago? It's early, we'll chip away. Things have come too easy, too early for KState. So, let's get things started by shutting them down on the next possession and we'll go from there.'"

Xavier did just that. Defensive pressure forced Kansas State into turnovers during their next few possessions while Xavier capitalized on clutch free throw shooting. By the next media timeout Xavier was still down nine, but stemmed the tide from earlier, and in a sense, was back in the game even though the score did not reflect it.

Mack said that even though his team was not closing the gap he saw one major difference between this game and the one played in December, "The same thing happened at the beginning of both games; KState did what they wanted on offense and disrupted us on defense. In the first game they got a big early lead and never looked back, but in this game I saw that we had withstood their first run and were not backing down. I could see in our player's eyes that the outcome of this game was going to be a lot different."

Xavier continued with defensive pressure and timely conversions on offense to finally take the lead on a Jamel McLean free throw to go into halftime with a one-point lead, 32-31. Mack saw the energy level was high in the locker room when he spoke to the team, "Fellas, we didn't play incredibly well, and we're up. In the second half continue to be the team you need to be; don't give up second shots and win the rebound battle. You have proven to yourselves in the latter part of the first half that we can be the better team. We won the last three wars that half, keep doing that this next half and we'll be fine."

The mood appeared different in the Kansas State locker room as CBS had cameras catch head coach Frank Martin yelling at his players about turnovers, "Guys it's silly! It's just silly!"

Mack spoke as he made his way back to the floor, "We had good percentages from the floor and the line in the first half, but so did KState. I really feel like this next half is simply a continuation of the first. We held our own on the boards, and that was huge. This won't be easy, but I like the look in our kids' eyes."

As expected Kansas State hung tough, scoring on their first possession to retake the lead. It was a lead that they would hold until a little over five minutes to go in the game. That was when Denis Clemente started to heat up for Kansas State.

"He is such a good player, and can light you up at any point during the game. Down the stretch he was making everything he put up," said Mack.

When Xavier forged out in front by a point, Clemente put the Wildcats ahead on the next possession. Xavier answered back when Jason Love scored down low to put Xavier back in the lead, but Clemente came through again. This time making a three-point shot in which he was fouled in the process of shooting. Making the free throw to complete the four-point play meant Clemente had scored the Wildcats last eight points.

Kansas State held a three point lead coming out of the last media timeout, but that was quickly erased by a clutch three-pointer from Dante Jackson. Kansas State retook the lead their next time down the floor when Curtis Kelly's jump shot went down. Jordan Crawford then hit a huge three to give Xavier the lead, but on the next play Jamel McLean fouled the Wildcats' Curtis Kelly sending him to the line for two shots. Kelly made the first of two, then missed the next.

When Kansas State grabbed a rebound with 47 seconds left, head coach Frank Martin called a timeout to set up a play for Jacob Pullen. The play worked when Pullen hit the apparent game winning shot, a three-pointer to put Kansas State up by three with just 26 seconds left.

Xavier quickly got the ball down the court to Terrell Holloway who was streaking towards the basket only to have his shot blocked, but Jason Love was there for the put back to cut the lead to one. Mack called timeout.

Mack wanted to give instructions for various end-of-game situations that were coming up; those went largely unheeded when Terrell Holloway fouled Jacob Pullen who went to the line and made both free throws. That put Kansas State back up by three with just 10 seconds left.

Mack again called a timeout to set up a tying three point play. As the players made their way to the bench Terrell Holloway came over to Mack and told him that he heard the Kansas State players saying they were going to foul.

Mack said of the situation, "There are a couple of different schools of thought when a team is up three and playing defense; do you foul and put the other team on the line for two shots, or do you let them play it out?

"When Terrell told me that he heard from the Kansas State players they were going to foul it helped. I thought if that was going to be the case, then we needed to get the ball to Terrell, he was our best free throw shooter all year."

When Xavier got the ball into Holloway's hands, Kansas State's

Chris Merriweather moved in. Holloway, knowing what he did, wanted to be in the act of shooting a three pointer, so that when he got fouled, he could go to the line for three shots and a chance to tie the game. Holloway went up with the ball to shoot, the whistle blew, and as hoped, Merriweather fouled Holloway.

Mack said of the play, "It was great instinct by Terrell, and a heads up play to know what KState was going to do. I looked out at him standing at the free throw line and had confidence that he could make all three. You know there are times, and that was certainly one of them, where there is nothing else you can do as a coach. It's all out of your hands. So, like everyone else I stood there and watched."

Holloway calmly made the first, then the second, before Frank Martin from Kansas State called timeout. When Mack's players came to the huddle he told them what to be prepared for after Holloway made the game-tying shot. "You have to talk as though the shot is going to be made, you can't present any other situation to your players, you never want to put any sort of doubt in their mind. I really did believe that after making the first two Terrell would make the third and that we needed to be aware of what to do on defense, KState still had time to score."

Holloway stepped to the line, went through his normal pre-shot routine and calmly made the last shot to tie the game. Kansas State got the ball inbounds quickly and up the floor to Jacob Pullen who took a long range three that missed. When Jason Love gathered in the rebound the horn sounded ending the game in regulation. Xavier had forced overtime.

Mack talked about getting ready for extra play, "I spoke with the assistants and we decided that there was no major foul trouble for either team, so nothing to worry about or exploit there. We just decided to keep going with some of the same sets that we used down the stretch and keep up the intensity on defense. We were really clicking on offense, so we felt that we could continue to do that in overtime."

When the ball was tipped for overtime the game now had a national audience since the late game in the East Regional between West Virginia and Washington was complete. The entire country was about to witness the most riveting basketball, not just of the NCAA Tournament, but of the entire year.

Xavier controlled the tip. Terrell Holloway quickly fed Jordan Crawford down low for a layup and the lead. As quickly as Xavier scored though, Curtis Kelly of Kansas State scored a layup and then was fouled on the next possession, making both free throws to put the Wildcats up by two. On Xavier's ensuing possession Jason Love missed his initial shot and then the put back was blocked by Curtis Kelly who was seemingly everywhere on the floor over the last minute of play. Jordan Crawford got the rebound, but missed his own shot that was recovered by Kansas State. When Jamar Samuels was fouled by Xavier's Andrew Taylor at the other end of the floor, his two made free throws had Kansas State in front by four, and threatening to put the game away.

The two teams traded field goals and free throws well into the last minute of play before Chris Merriweather of Kansas State was fouled with 19 seconds to play. Kansas State was up by two and had a chance to widen the lead. Merriweather made the first, but missed the second. Xavier got the rebound and Mack called for timeout.

Everyone in the arena knew the ball was going to be in Jordan Crawford's hands, "It's tough when you have so little time and your opponent knows you need a three to tie, but we had put Jordan in those situations all year long. We just needed him to do what he had done all season one more time."

When Xavier got the ball to Crawford he came over the time line, but was having a hard time getting clear for a shot, "KState decided they would give us a two point basket if we decided, so they over-committed way beyond the three point line. It really disrupted what we wanted to do on offense and consequently a lot of time was running off the clock," Mack said of the final possession.

As the clock wound down to 6 seconds left, Crawford finally broke free and let a three pointer fly from ten feet beyond the arc. The ball seemed to hang in the air forever before finally crawling over the front of the rim and into the basket.

Game tied, 87-87.

The arena erupted as Gus Johnson on CBS was beside himself giving the play by play, "Crawford's gotta hurry, OHHHHH, AHH-HHH!!! He tied it!!"

Mack said of the play, "You know at that point I just wanted to make sure we had the presence of mind to get back and play defense. Clemente got the ball down the court quickly and was able to get off a pretty good shot, but fortunately for us, he missed, and we got to play for another five minutes.

"You know I remember thinking at that point that I have this group of kids that no matter what will not quit. There were so many times up to that moment where the fans or the team on the other bench thought we were done, but we just kept swinging."

Mack said of the second overtime, "What was really hard about the first overtime was that Kansas State scored on every possession except the miss by Clemente at the end. We were scoring on our end, but could not stop them on defense. I knew that couldn't last in the second overtime, and that we needed to lock down on defense."

The teams traded baskets until Xavier had a dead ball inbounds under their own basket with a little over a minute and a half to go with the score tied 91-91. Mack called for a play that he felt could put Xavier ahead for good, "We had a special play that we ran all year where we put Jordan just off the ball in the paint, so that the man guarding him was sort of caught between looking at Jordan and looking at the ball. Many times we will run Jordan off a set of screens to try and get open for a shot, so that defender is waiting to get on his horse and follow Jordan.

"The wrinkle in this play was that if our man inbounding the ball, in this case Dante Jackson, saw that the defender was not even looking at the ball he would signal for a quick pass. We saw things setting up for this play and signaled in the play. When Dante got the ball from the referee he instantly threw it in to Jordan, whose defender was caught unaware. Jordan scored an easy two to give the lead, and I really felt at the time like it gave us the momentum we needed to stay in the lead for the last minute of the game."

Kansas State however would not be denied, and on their next possession Jacob Pullen buried another three-pointer to go ahead by one. It was a dagger to the heart from which Xavier would not recover. After a Jason Love free throw tied the game, Pullen drained another long range bomb to put Kansas State up by three with 32 seconds to play.

Kansas State fouled the wrong man, Terrell Holloway, on Xavier's next possession, who again calmly went to the line and made both free throws to cut the lead to one with 25 seconds left.

Mack gathered his team in the huddle with the first directive being not to foul on Kansas State's next possession until Kansas State crossed half-court. Mack's thinking was that Kansas State was expecting to get fouled, and therefore would be slowly bringing the ball up the court. So by throwing the curveball of not fouling, it might force Kansas State to lose their poise by hurrying up to get the over the timeline, and possibly commit a turnover in the process.

Unfortunately, Mark Lyons did not get the message and quickly fouled Jacob Pullen. Mack said, "It was unfortunate that Cheeks made that foul, but we had to move on."

Pullen made both free throws to give Kansas a three point lead. Xavier got the ball into the hands of Dante Jackson who got off a three point shot, but missed. Kansas State got the rebound with 12 seconds to play. Denis Clemente made the first free throw before Mack called his last timeout of the season. "We told our kids what we wanted to do off a make or miss. I knew at that point it was slipping away, but you play until you hear the buzzer. I had already seen crazier things happen that night, so you never knew what could happen in the last ten seconds, which is still a lot of time."

Clemente made the second, so Xavier, with no timeouts left and down by five points, came down the floor needing to make a three just to have a chance, but came up short when Jordan Crawford missed from out top. The miss sent the ball into Brad Redford's hands who threw up a meaningless desperation three that rattled out.

That was it, it was over, Kansas State had won 101-96.

Mack said, "I went over and shook Frank's hand and told him his kids played a great game and good luck on Saturday against Butler. I was really down walking off the court. I knew at the time it was such an amazing game, and people were trying to be nice patting you on the back and telling you how great you did, but it just couldn't change the fact that we had just lost. The season was over."

Many wonder what it is like to coach in a game that intense, and question whether or not a coach like Mack gets caught up in the moment, "You certainly live the highs and lows of the game while it's going on. You try to separate your emotions to be able to put your players in the best position that you can, both offensively and defensively. It's tough.

"But we always tell our kids to have a next-play mentality. It's what you have to do as a coach. While we're on the defensive end, you're trying to think what you want to run offensively the next time you get the ball. Again, it teetered back and forth. But we could never build on the lead. We were always trying to recapture the lead. And that's tough."

Mack's wife Christi said shortly afterwards, "What an unbelievable game. I thought the kids were great all night, they never backed down, there was never an ounce of quit in them. I just feel so bad for them, they poured everything into tonight. I am worn out. I can't imagine how much this game took out of the players, Chris, and the staff."

Ironically enough, a week later while attending the Final Four, Christi found herself running side by side Frank Martin on a treadmill at the hotel. Christi introduced herself to Martin, who immediately launched into a recap of the game. Christi said that Martin had commented to her that, "That game took so much out of our team it was incredible. Consequently we weren't able to elevate to that same level two nights later against Butler. We about gave all we had just to get by Xavier."

The locker room was quiet afterwards with a lot of tears. When Mack entered though his spirits had lifted a bit, "Once I was off the court and down the tunnel, and it was just our team, I reflected on so many of the moments during the game where the tide had swung, and that we just never backed down. I had a real sense of pride when I got up in front of the kids afterwards."

Each of the players and coaches looked to Mack, "Fellas I just want to tell you that I could not have a better group of guys to coach. I can't begin to say what a joy it was to lead a group that believed in themselves and their first year coach. That was an unbelievable game, national TV, and so on, a game we could have won. That was fun. As much as it hurts right now I can't but help and think back to something my old high school coach, Dick Berning, used to tell our team after a tough loss to end the year, 'no matter how tough this is, and no matter how horrible you feel, the sun will come up tomorrow. This will pass.'"

Mack slowly made his way to each player in the room and thanked them for all of their effort during the year. Some were tougher than others. Mack had tears in his own eyes when he spoke to senior Jason Love.

Love knew that he had just played his last game as a Musketeer, and would never don the blue and white uniform again. Mack said, "It's always toughest on the seniors. I think when you are a junior or an underclassman there is that feeling of 'we'll get it again next year.' But when you're a senior it's a really empty feeling. All I could say to Jason was that I thanked him for who he had been for four years and that I was proud of him for the effort."

Mack wanted a few minutes to collect himself before facing the media; it had been a long night. With his two daughters standing by his side, Mack looked over the stat sheet for the last time, looked up and said, "I've only been involved with another game like that before one time, which was a North Carolina/Wake Forest triple overtime game. Certainly the stakes weren't as high. I felt like tonight was eerily similar to Ali/Foreman, and they landed the last punch, unfortunately. As good of a game as I've coached, or been a part of. Both teams battled and believed they were going to win. Unfortunately, only one team is allowed to. Have to credit Jacob Pullen. He's a tremendous player. I love that kid. I don't like him right now, but big-time guts."

With a little more emotion Mack added, "I love my kids. Toughness, grit. There were several times I felt we could have folded but we kept fighting. I'm just disappointed for them, especially Jason."

Afterword

The team's arrival back to Cincinnati was a little less glorious than the week before after beating Pittsburgh. After the loss to Kansas State the team quietly gathered up their things and headed to the hotel where they stayed the night before a charter flight home in the morning.

When Mack awoke the pain was still there, "There's always a certain feeling of finality of your season no matter where or when it ends. You get so wrapped up in the movement from one game to the next, and focus on getting your team prepared as best they can. Then all of the sudden, it's over."

A long, quiet plane ride back to Cincinnati was followed by a quick bus trip to the Cintas Center. It was no surprise to anyone on the team that there was going to be a brief meeting in the locker room when the team got back. Mack wanted to touch on a couple of topics that he felt needed to be addressed now, in person, instead of later in the media. At the top of that list; what was going to happen with Jordan Crawford.

There had been talk as the season wore on that Crawford had the potential to be selected in the upcoming NBA draft in June. With Crawford's performance in the NCAA Tournament, talk of his draft status went from a possibility to projecting whether or not he would be a first round pick. During the year, as many around the game became aware of the type of player Crawford was turning out to be, the initial thought was that if Crawford continued to perform at that level for the remainder of the year he might go in the second round. After getting a fair amount of national exposure during Xavier's run to the Sweet 16, Crawford was now being projected as a low first round pick.

The program faced a similar situation a year ago when Derrick Brown was deciding on whether or not to enter the draft. The issue was compounded by Sean Miller's leaving for Arizona. Consequently, there was a void for the players of not knowing what was going on with their teammate, let alone their team. Mack wanted to address Crawford's situation immediately, "Having learned from the Derrick Brown situation a year earlier I decided to get it out in the open at that time because I really felt that he was going to have the opportunity come his way, and we might as well address it as a team now instead of in the 11th hour when it happened."

Mack said at the time, "Plus, this year we didn't have the added distraction regarding the head coach. I wasn't going anywhere, so in my mind, it was the only potential disruptive item that I thought we needed to discuss. It was not a secret; we all knew it was probably coming, no point hiding from it."

Mack wasted no time getting to the point when he stood in front of the team, "There is going to be a lot of talk regarding Jordan over the next few weeks and he has a tough decision on his hands. If he decides to go into the draft we will look quite different as a team moving forward. I know as his coach I want to see nothing but the best for him, I know we all do, so let's support him through this. We'll know soon enough and go from there."

Mack spoke to the team about what was going to happen over the next month before the summer break. The staff went over workout schedules, expectations of players during the spring, and what lie ahead in the off-season. The team stood together in a circle for the last time of the season as Mack closed things down by saying, "Fellas I'm proud of the way you handled yourselves all year long, and I look forward to our next season together. Let's stay focused the last month of school, and then spend the time this spring working on your game, getting better and stronger. Finally, remember, your actions reflect on everyone in this room, so make sure you make good decisions and take care of yourselves."

With that the team broke the circle and started cleaning out their lockers before heading back to their dorms. It wasn't that the staff and players were not going to see each other the next month that school was in session, but per NCAA rules, practice was over until next year.

When Mack got to his office he sat down on the couch, looked through the windows, and gazed down on the court where so much time was spent during the last twelve months. Mack had completed his first year as head coach, and by most people's standards, had done quite well. The team continued to win, not only in the conference, but in the NCAA Tournament, as many had done in the program before Mack's arrival.

Mack briefly reflected on his first year, "You know, overall I have to say I'm pleased. We accomplished my main goal at the beginning of the year; to be a better team by the end of the year." When the dust finally settled on the 2009-2010 basketball season, many of the teams Xavier faced during the year had varied outcomes, as well as the two players that had moved on from the program:

Dayton Flyers- after being bounced by Xavier in the quarterfinals of the A-10 Championship the Flyers did not get an at-large invite to the NCAA Tournament. Their season however was far from over. After being invited to the NIT, the Flyers went on a winning streak that took them all the way to the championship game against North Carolina. Dayton ended their year with a win, defeating the Tar Heels to claim the first NIT championship in school history.

Richmond Spiders- the team sparred with Xavier all year long atop the standings in the A-10. Richmond lost to Temple in the conference championship finals, but made it into the NCAA. Richmond's stay was short lived though; they were upset by St. Mary's in the first round 80-71.

Kansas State Wildcats- after beating Xavier in what was considered the best game of the year, the Wildcats couldn't summon enough energy two days later when they lost to Butler 63-56.

Butler Bulldogs- the Bulldogs were headed home for the Final Four after their win against Kansas State. After getting by a tough Michigan State team the Bulldogs' dream of winning a national championship in their hometown ended when Gordon Hayward's half-court shot glanced off the rim as the final horn sounded.

Cincinnati Bearcats- Xavier's hometown nemesis struggled since losing the Crosstown Shootout to Xavier in mid-December, eventually ending the year with a home loss to Dayton in the NIT.

Jason Love- the senior center who will undoubtedly go down as one of the most prominent players in Xavier history was not selected in the NBA draft the following June. Love's playing days were not over though as he was invited to a number of NBA tryouts before getting the opportunity to sign on with the Philadelphia 76ers to play on their summer league team. Love's time on the court was short lived when he tore his ACL midway through the summer, thus ending his playing time for the immediate future. Love would have the surgery in Philadelphia and rehab there before planning on coming back to Xavier to get his master's degree and be involved once again with the basketball program.

Jordan Crawford- was selected in the NBA draft as the 27th pick in the first round by the New Jersey Nets. Later in the evening Crawford was traded to the Atlanta Hawks.

The last time we saw Chris Mack on this journey was a solitary moment shooting baskets by himself at the Cintas Center working up a good sweat. Even though it was midsummer, Mack was already thinking about the season ahead, "Next year is a new year, our record is 0-0 and we have a lot to work on. We'll have two notable absences in both Jason and Jordan, but I am really excited about the new kids we have coming in. October will be here before we know it, and I can't wait to get back into the swing of things."

Mack's workout was halted by the sound of his cell phone ringing, it was his wife Christi. Like many wives, she wanted to know what time her husband would be home for dinner. Mack said he would be on his way shortly.

Mack looked up, grinned, and said, "Gotta go, workout's over."

As Mack turned out the lights at the Cintas Center and walked out the side door, he had a bit of a hurry in his step as he headed toward his car. Not only did he have to get home, but he needed to watch some game film from the past season because he wanted to tweak a few things on offense for the upcoming season.

For Mack there is always a sense of urgency, and of course, he needed to watch film because, "The first practice is less than 60 days away!"

About the Author

Scott Gaede is a sports enthusiast and writer from Cincinnati, Ohio, where he lives with his wife and two children. Scott graduated from St. Xavier High School in 1988 before enrolling at the University of Evansville. For several years, he worked for NBC Sports where he covered major golf events. His first book, *The Open Road: Five Years at the U.S. Open with NBC Sports* is a recollection of his behind-the-scenes experiences with the legendary event and golf's finest players (available by sending a request to sjgaede@gmail.com). *Next in Line* is his second book, chronicling the first year of Head Coach Chris Mack at Xavier University.